Guerrilla Teambuilding

A Project Management Guide for Creating and
Managing Effective Workgroups

John F. Zagotta, Psy.D.

J. F. Zagotta & Associates, LLC
8700 W. Bryn Mawr, Suite 800 S
Chicago, IL 60631

www.jfzassoc.com

Published Through:
BookSurge, LLC
An Amazon Company
www.booksurge.com
1-866-308-6235

Disclaimers:

Although written by a clinical psychologist, this book does not in any way constitute clinical advice. Clinical direction and treatment can only be provided in direct care following a full assessment. Any persons seeking such clinical direction must seek out the services of a behavioral health professional.

Although this book provides parameters of business and organizational strategy, it is not a substitute for direct business management consultation services. No guarantees of outcome can be given and results will vary.

Contents

Contents

Contents

Contents

Exercises

Figures

Contents

Illustrations

Contents

Implementation Checklists

Worksheets

Acknowledgements

I am indebted to all of the extraordinary professionals that have been teammates of mine. It has been a pleasure to serve with them and learn from them. They include the staff of the former Diamond Star Motor's Assessment Center, Normal, IL (a Towers, Perrin, Forester, and Crosby consulting project); the Orland Township Youth Services, Orland Park, IL; the Graduate Psychology Department at Illinois State University, Normal, IL; the Health Psychology Program at the Illinois School of Professional Psychology, Chicago, IL; the State University of New York at Buffalo Counseling Center, Amherst, NY; the Child and Adolescent Services Division of the Madison Center and Hospital, South Bend, IN; J.D. Maher & Associates, Inc., Joliet, IL; as well as the emergency services staffs of Loreto Hospital, Chicago, IL; and Resurrection Healthcare, Chicago, IL. My experiences as a member of these teams have shaped and crystallized my concept of team, and my confidence in the power of the team process.

My deepest thanks and gratitude to my partner, Angela Lew, Ph.D., without whose encouragement, support, and patience this work would not have been possible.

Chapter One

Introduction

This Guerilla Teambuilding **(GT)** guide will provide the reader with a ready-to-use outline for establishing effective teams.

Especially in today's hyper-productive business environment, effective teams represent the essential mechanism for deploying highly skilled, but costly, labor resources. Like flexible manufacturing processes, these human resources must be developed to agilely recombine with others and produce custom-tailored skill sets that satisfy transitory business requirements. Such enriched resources become ever more effective, as each new project experience heightens their ability to leverage the broader skill sets of the collective team.

Once practiced at these advanced techniques, team players can be expected to operate the same way throughout the business practice. The result is a dynamic, shifting application of all available business skills, intelligently focused and integrated to resolve ever-changing requirements. And the impact can be especially dramatic when these highly effective teams focus their efforts on resolving customer requirements.

Guerilla Teams aren't just "nice to have". They are essential:

- **Guerilla Teams** provide a competitive edge.

- **Guerilla Teams are truly more than the sum of their parts,** are much more effective than individuals and are infinitely more effective than groups of people who do not work as a team or work poorly as one.

- **Today's economy calls for the work of time-limited and highly focused Guerilla Teams**, formed at need, to manage and execute various projects, then dissolve, with all members going to join new teams.

- **The individual's ability to join a Guerilla Team** effectively (being able to enter, contribute and re-enter ongoing projects) will be a crucial skill in future working environments, according to Daniel Goleman (*Working with Emotional Intelligence,* 1998, Bantam Books).

- **The entertainment industry** (according to Goleman), which is organized around such highly productive, time-limited Guerilla Teams, serves as a model for the future workplace organization.

- **Foundations for** understanding and implementing the strategies put forth in Guerrilla Teambuilding **(GT)** are referenced at the end of this guide:
  1. **Daniel Goleman** (*Emotional Intelligence*, *Working with Emotional Intelligence* and *Primal Leadership*)
  2. **Mihaly Csikszentmihalyi** (*Flow*)
  3. **Isabel Briggs Myers** (*Introduction to Type*)

What Makes a Team a Guerrilla Team (GT)?

We have all had the experience of being members of a team, and it is likely that we are all currently members of several different teams.

- **Some of these are memorable** experiences, but **some are not**.

- **For those that are** — what made them that way?

- **The ones that stood out** likely possessed some aspects of the Guerrilla Teambuilding **(GT)** program.

The essence of a Guerilla Team is the integration of team members' intents and efforts, and the shared reliance on the combined strengths of the team. The purposeful nature of Guerilla Team projects focuses all team member efforts toward that defined goal. All team members are held available to contribute their individual strengths to all team efforts. By jointly identifying team member strengths, all team members become familiar with the "catalog" of skill sets available for application to each project task. Each team member is empowered to rely on the known strengths of all other team members, either for specific project task activities or for skill / knowledge transfer to achieve personal development. Essentially, each team member is endowed with the much larger skill sets of the broader team.

Key Characteristics of the Guerrilla Team (GT) Approach

The following are key characteristics that define the **(GT)** approach.

- **The actual term "guerrilla"** derives from the Spanish word *guerra*, meaning *war*. It is ultimately of Latin derivation and similar in all Romance languages.

- **Guerrilla denotes a small fighting force** that utilizes intensive and unconventional tactics to gain an advantage against a larger opponent.

- **The (GT) model provides a competitive advantage** by relying on these special tactics, not an organization's size, financial backing or technological advantages.

- **The major tactics** of Guerrilla Teambuilding include:
  - leveraging members' strengths,
  - embracing and orchestrating member diversity, and, in doing so,
  - promoting the peak performance state known as *Flow*.

- **A Guerrilla Team is about organizational structure.** It is not simply the promotion of "goodwill" and / or "empathy" for one's teammates.

- **The Guerrilla Teambuilding (GT) program reclaims teambuilding** endeavors away from the "soft-skill" / relationship model. **(GT)** focuses instead on the implementation of tangible organizational structures that promote optimal productivity and team member satisfaction.

- **In these globally competitive times,** organizations large and small must find competitive ways to reinvent themselves and to retain talented workers. Both productivity and worker satisfaction are critical success factors.

Guerrilla Teams (GT) Are Much Better Than Ordinary Teams

Following are a few examples that highlight the distinction between ordinary teams and Guerrilla Teams.

- **Guerrilla Teams maximize efficiency and productivity** when accomplishing tasks.

- **Guerrilla Teams emphasize and achieve** a rewarding work experience for their members.

- **Guerrilla Teams are primarily organized around the Human Resources**, or assets, of the team members. Other supports, resources and technologies are of secondary importance.

- **Guerrilla Teams can be successful in any setting**, because their basic functioning components are people. An organization need not make an exorbitant financial investment to create such teams. Definitive support and organizational context are the only necessary investment.

- **Guerrilla Teams exist to accomplish specific goals,** not for arbitrary reasons. Once the goals of the team have been accomplished, either new assignments are given to the team, or the resources of the team (its members) disperse to assist in other organizational endeavors.

- **Guerrilla Teams form and disband** as required.

- **Guerrilla Teams utilize interactive, integrated processes**. Each member's skills are enhanced by their ability to leverage the skills of other team members. As a result, all members of the Guerrilla Team become better at what they do. Guerilla Teams are not simply people housed in a similar location, or with similar job functions or assignments.

- **Guerrilla Teams have interchangeable component pieces** and skills that make their efforts easily repeatable.

- **Guerilla Teams are adaptable,** dynamically adjusting team makeup and work breakdown with these components, based on the specific current project activity requirements.

- **Guerrilla Teambuilding's ultimate success** depends upon combining the component parts of the **(GT)** program to facilitate the peak performance state known as *Flow* within team processes.

- **Guerrilla Teams function to promote and optimize the *Flow* state** within its processes. This generates the tactical advantage of the Guerrilla Team model.

- **Guerrilla Teams operate on a win / win basis within organizations.** What is positive and growth-promoting for the individual is also positive and growth-promoting for the greater organization — in terms of efficiency, productivity, and financial returns.

- **Guerilla Teams stress inter-reliance** on the broader strengths and skill sets of the overall team.

- **Guerilla Teambuilding (GT) is a process** that redefines the work approach for team members, vastly enhancing the reach and impact of each individual.

Use of this guide

This **(GT)** guide will divide the discussion of Guerrilla Teambuilding **(GT)** into the following steps:

- The Case for Adoption of Guerrilla Teambuilding [Chapter 2]

- The "Visual Operations Plan" (VOP) [Chapter 3]

- Team Structure and Communication [Chapter 4]

- Know the Team / Know the Coach [Chapter 5]

- The OHIO, *Flow* and OTF Management Models [Chapter 6]

- Guerrilla Team Case Study: "The Starship Enterprise" [Chapter 7]

The **(GT)** guide is specifically designed for:

- **Any individual charged with creating teams** and making teams work effectively.

- **Managers and higher-level organizational leaders** seeking insight into effective organizational teambuilding.

- **Professionals and potential team members** seeking insight into what a supervisor (coach) may look for and how to function as a more effective (and sought after) team member.

The purpose of this **(GT)** guide is to:

- **Give the reader** an *immediate* and *proven* model for establishing teams.

- **Dramatically reduce** the *learning curve* for effective teambuilding endeavors.

- **Integrate Approaches Known to Bring Success.** The current guide is a synthesis of central and accepted ideas found in many standard business and organizational practices.

The **(GT)** program has two key components that are external to most organizations:

- **The use of professional** coaches / consultants.

- **The appropriate usage** of accepted *psychometric inventories* by trained professionals.

This **(GT)** guide provides an abundance of tools to assist implementation:

- **Checklists and other quick reference tools** serve as guidelines and practice sessions for use in developing your **(GT)** program.

- **These resources appear** at the end of each chapter.

- **They are designed to be separately reproducible** for the purchasers of this guide in direct applications (but not for mass distribution).

Chapter Two

The Case for Adoption

Of the Guerrilla Teambuilding Approach

The approaches outlined in this guide hold great utility for maximizing the interactive potential of any team, even the most successful ones. Probably, you need to take action. This chapter delineates diagnostic indicators of this need and provides a set of approaches to achieve resolution.

However, Guerrilla Teambuilding **(GT)** is not just a problem resolution mechanism. As discussed in **Chapter One**, **(GT)** is a new technique for integrating the work processes of all employees – with exceptional benefits in three major areas:

1. **Focus.** Guerrilla Teams work toward common, defined results. Team members self-regulate all team activity toward these goals.
2. **Efficiency.** Guerrilla Team members become adept at applying the best available skill set to specific task requirements. This approach reduces the "wrong tool for the job" inefficiencies.
3. **Productivity.** Guerilla Teams do more, because they have more with which to work. Individuals are not constrained by their own limitations; they can leverage the fuller skill sets of the team.

The **(GT)** process, once established, fosters a new approach to all work efforts. With team members accustomed to inter-reliance, they expand the approach to cover all their responsibilities. The effect is to "turbo-charge" daily work efforts.

The **Focus** employed during transitory project assignments engenders habits of task definition and urgency. Since project tasks are interdependent, Guerrilla Team members are always striving to complete one task in order to get to the next. Instead of simply plodding through repetitive paperwork, a Guerrilla Team member asks "What am I trying to do, here?" Inevitably, the Guerrilla Team member begins seeking ways to accomplish the task more quickly.

This same sense of urgency, coupled with the habit of inter-reliance, compels the Guerrilla Team member to "use the right tool" – in everything they do. "I shouldn't be doing this. John knows a better way." **Efficiency** becomes an organizational imperative.

In the pursuit of almost every immediate goal, every worker recognizes additional needs. An individual is often forced to admit "I can't worry about that, right now." A Guerrilla Team member, however, has formed the habit of dependency on teammates. Their response is most likely to be "I better tell Samantha about this." Organizational **Productivity** is improved.

But **(GT)** benefits are not limited to long-term organizational impacts. The **(GT)** approach is of immediate value to you as a supervisor or manager if you would answer yes to one or more of the following questions.

- **Maximizing All Workers' Potentials.** Do you have employees in your work group who do not seem to *shine*? Do you have employees who <u>do</u> display a particular "strength" related to their current work group assignments or functions? Have you made efforts for these two groups to help each other?

- **Effective Communication.** Do you feel 20% or more of your time is spent sorting out disagreements or "personality issues" among the employees in your work group?

- **Complaining Versus Problem Solving.** Is 20% or more of your work group's meeting time preoccupied with repetitive complaints that never seem to get resolved?

- **Unresolved Issues.** Do the majority of employees in your work group recurrently voice the same legitimate complaints about specific assignments or responsibilities that never seem to get resolved?

- **Limits to Productivity.** Do you as a supervisor or manager feel your work group's effectiveness and productivity remain limited by problems with integrating interpersonal differences and backgrounds? Could these challenges account for more than 20% of your productivity shortfall?

- **Employee Satisfaction.** Would 60% or fewer of the employees in your work group state that they generally find their work assignments gratifying?

- **Management of Human Resources.** Do you as a supervisor or manager feel that despite sufficient technological and financial resources, as well as adequate upper management support, your work group still continues to fall short of its goals or has not optimized its potential?

The 1/5 Call to Action

Note that in the questions listed above, the figure 20% (or 1/5) is used repeatedly as a cut-off or action-trigger.

- **Time Investment.** If 1/5 of your time or more is spent on a particular problem area, then this area warrants special attention.

- **Efficiency and Satisfaction.** If an action could increase efficiency by 1/5, or reduce time spent in an unpleasant work assignment by 1/5, then these areas are worth special efforts.

- **Benchmark.** This 1/5 rule provides an easy marker for targeting the productivity, profit and problem opportunities that are worthwhile pursuits.

- **The Benefits of Action.** If a problem exists, or a gain can be made at this level, significant positive changes are a likely result. Action should be taken to *minimize the problem* and *maximize the strengths*.

To illustrate the *1/5 Call to Action*, here are tangible measures of 20% values.

- **Tangible Time Cut-Off.** 1/5 of a standard work day is 1.6 hours.

- **Time is Money.** Ask yourself if you can afford to be unproductive for 1½ or 2 hours a day in your current work assignment. Can you afford to have the employees in your work group unproductive for the same amount of time?

- **Routine Waste.** Most of us are already unproductive for 1½ to 2 hours a day.

- **Waste on Top of Waste.** A bad scenario is to experience this down time when you actually intend to be productive. It's even worse when this comes on top of the 1½ to 2 hours a day that are already unproductive.

- **Widgets = Dollars.** This *Call to Action* can also be viewed from a productivity or dollars perspective.

- **Tangible Dollars Lost.** If your work group produces the equivalent of 1 million dollars of revenue each year, a 1/5 increase would be $200,000 in profits. Conversely, the current opportunity represents a $200,000 loss that your work group is causing.

- **Tangible Dollars Gained.** You could also document this $200,000 increase in terms of a 1/5 savings or increase in efficiency. You can do the math yourself for larger figures.

- **Cut-Off Points Made Tangible.** If you think about these 1/5 cut-off points with reference to time intervals or dollar amounts, they provide tangible examples of what constitute a good *Call to Action* point or *level of significance*[i] for your specific endeavors.

The 80/20 Rule

This rule has a number of common applications, but I focus on its usage in the area of workplace productivity. For that purpose, the rule goes something like this:

- **The Few Do the Most.** 80% of all the work gets done by 20% of the employees.

- **The Most Do the Least.** The remaining 20% of the work is accomplished by the remaining 80% of the employees.

- **The Few Ruin the Most.** An extension to this adage would posit that 80% of the problems that occur in a work setting are caused by 20% of the people who work there.

- **The Few Don't Ruin the Most.** The remaining 20% of those problems are the result of efforts by the remaining 80% of employees.

- **Superstars.** A few star performers usually carry the operation.

- **Underachievement.** The majority of employees do not contribute what they might towards accomplishing goals.

- **One Bad Apple.** Often, most of the problems in a work setting can be attributed to a small group of individuals termed star *problem makers*.

None of these situations are likely to be a constant condition. However, these 80/20 observations are probably apparent — in spurts and cycles — in most organizations. In fact, the cyclical presentation of these types of situations is the most common type of occurrence. These conditions represent a major management challenge, and **(GT)** is a systemic way to resolve them.

- **Management – The Prevention and the Cure.** Effective management can keep this dynamic from rearing its head. And effective management can remedy this condition when it does emerge.

- **The Right Tool…** The Guerrilla Teambuilding **(GT)** program is a specific management tool that can help interrupt this cycle of 80/20 conditions.

If you don't see truth in these assumptions or you don't see these scenarios played out amongst the employees that you supervise or manage (as well as within your supervisory and managerial colleagues), then you must have an optimally efficient, productive and satisfying work environment.

- **You May Already Use (GT).** If that's the case, the approaches outlined in Guerrilla Teambuilding may already guide your work environment. Or, perhaps, your work environment does not require improvement via these specialized approaches.

- **You May Not Need to Initiate (GT), but** this guide will allow you to identify these admirable processes within your organization. By recognizing exactly what you are doing right, you can use any of the tools provided in this **(GT)** guide to begin a conscious organizational effort to "emphasize the positive" and build on these strengths.

If your organization is like most, then this 80/20 rule probably does seem relevant to your supervisory or managerial situation. That's actually good news, because you are already holding an effective tool to address the immediate problem – and reap significant long-term benefits for your organization. The Guerrilla Teambuilding approach should prove immensely helpful to you.

- **80/20 Holds True For Star Performers.** If you <u>do</u> find that something like 20% of the people do 80% of the work…

- **80/20 Holds True for Non-Star Performers.** If you also find a different 20% of the people cause around 80% (or a vast majority) of the problems in your work setting,

- **You May Need (GT).** You also probably answered yes to most or all of the questions at the beginning of this chapter.

- **Some Additional Guidelines.** Assuming that these issues do resonate for you, the following sub-sections will help you to immediately begin addressing the issue. These provide insights and strategies that can be used, right now, to start moving in a better direction. The rest of this Guerrilla Teambuilding **(GT)** guide will build on those foundations.

80/20 Distribution

The 80/20 rule can be explained by means of the bell curve.

- **All populations can be divided into groupings.** Every group has an upper end of a distribution, a lower end and a middle – or average – group. It's just about where the cut-offs are assigned.

- **Extremes of performance are expected.** Given this rule of expected distribution, we see extremes (or notable differences) at either end across specific performance areas (in this case, employee productivity).

- **The middle has less variation.** The middle 60% contributes less intense outcomes (either positive or negative) than the two extreme ends.

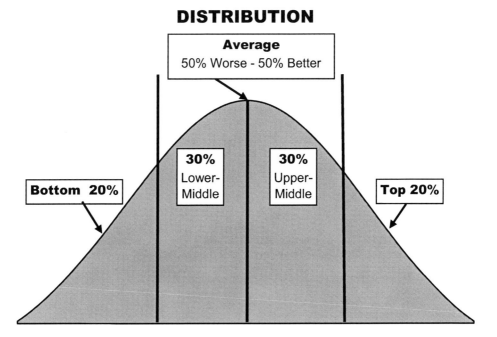

DISTRIBUTION

Therefore, there are three basic methods to improve work productivity, efficiency and satisfaction:

1. Maximize the top 20%

2. Minimize and improve the bottom 20%

3. Enhance the middle 60%

Maximizing the top 20%

- **Don't round-out or balance these top performers' assignments.** Their peak performance is not likely to generalize, so keep them with their strengths and preferences.

- **Leave their responsibilities alone.** They are probably top performers because they are functioning from their strengths and preferences and for the most part they are not asked to do things they don't enjoy or are not good at.

- **Leverage their strengths.** Give the top performers the resources to help them improve upon these areas of peak performance.

- **Orchestrate their strengths.** Pair top performers with people of complementary, but not identical strengths.

- **Minimize the weaknesses of others.** Pair them with people who either hate to do, or are not good at doing, what these peak performers do well.

Minimizing and improving the bottom 20%

- **This might not be remediable**. At the extreme lower end of this group, the skills required to perform the tasks assigned to the work group may be beyond an employee's ability or motivation.

- **Don't beat a dead horse!** These people are more likely, however, to be matched with assignments they do not enjoy and / or have little ability for.

- **Lead with their strengths.** In an explorative process, figure out what these employees are good at or enjoy, and then reassign responsibilities accordingly.

- **Leverage strengths and minimize weaknesses.** Two or more people paired with differing and complementary strengths and weaknesses can make all the difference in the world, and consequently, form an unbeatable team!

- **Find a *fitting* home.** Maybe the tasks and responsibilities in your work group are not good fits (ability or preference wise) for these individuals. Work with these employees using your organization's resources (fellow supervisors and managers, Human Resource Department) to identify areas that are good *fits* for them.

- **Don't write them off!** Because these employees *display* (as opposed to *possess* — it's about fit, not necessarily about ability) the most notable current performance deficits, changes in their performance can bring about the most profound returns on your time and efforts. *A little change in this group can make a big impact!*

Enhancing the middle 60%

- **Always find the *fit*.** There are gains to be made when one creates a fit of ability and preferences with work assignments and responsibilities. Especially with this large group, fine tailoring of assignments toward strengths and preferences are likely to reap large gains in productivity.

- **Diamonds in the *middle*.** To find the greatest potential for positive change, look at the persons with whom these employees are paired or teamed and assess whether this middle group has the ability to leverage the strengths (or minimize the weaknesses) of others.

- **Flexible and balanced.** This group represents a well-balanced and more easily adjustable preference and / or ability base. They will adjust more readily and respond more productively to carefully crafted pairings or responsibility changes.

- **Orchestrate. Orchestrate. Orchestrate.** Pair or team members of this group with those who will complement their strengths and preferences well. Remember that there are two productive matchings. Either increase / maximize notable strengths (abilities and preferences). Or minimize notable challenges (once again, preferences, abilities or both).

80/20 Hoop Dreams

Let's consider the implications of the 80/20 Principle by exploring some basketball analogies. Basketball is a rich source of illustration. You can probably name a few obvious examples yourself. For example, Wilt Chamberlain may have been the most dominant basketball player ever. But we know that Wilt scoring 50+ points did not necessarily mean his team won the game. His dominance did not mean that he was on the team that won the most championships. As another example, look at the most recent USA Olympic dream team. Clearly, this was a group of top 20% players. But they failed to orchestrate their efforts and got "creamed" by a group of middle 60% players that *did* orchestrate well.

For in-depth analogies, the Chicago Bulls of the 1990's and the Los Angeles Lakers of the first half of the 2000's are most instructive. Take a look at the following team breakdown. We might quibble over the category assignments, but you get the drift.

Bulls Talent Distribution on Championship Teams

Top 20%	Middle 60% (Maximized)	Botom20% (role players)
Jordan	Grant	Kerr
Pipen	Paxson	Hodges
	Kucoc	Longley
	Rodman(?)	Cartwright(?)

Michael Jordan was arguably the greatest overall player ever. For years Jordan was the most exciting player to watch, was the best by far — highest scorer, greatest slam dunks, etc. But he played on a mediocre-to-losing team, because he had no supporting cast — or at least not an orchestrated supporting cast. The Bulls did not win championships until the middle 60% and the bottom 20% started scoring. Jordan and the Bulls won games when a broad number of players were in double digits, not when he was over 30 points. A well rounded team scoring effort was their predictor of success. Jordan was a superstar who didn't win until he had a well-rounded team supporting him, and leveraging his strengths. He made them better — because Michael could do the really hard stuff. They made him better — because he didn't have to do everything.

The Bulls succeeded by establishing dual threats on the floor. Scottie Pippen could also drive the lane. John Paxson, Craig Hodges, Steve Curr and Tony Kucoc were deadly outside shooters. And a succession of strong tall men could be fed the ball under the net, men like Horace Grant, Bill Cartwright, and Luc Longley. In essence, you had to guard everybody. And it made Jordan that much more of the ultimate offensive weapon. Remember the basic Bulls' offense — it wasn't run and gun. They got down to half-court, set up, and passed the ball "at least three times". Three passes was pure formula; it got everyone into the game, it made every man on the court a scoring threat. It worked (with 6 championships to prove it)!
The Bulls were even contenders the two years that Jordan was out, because the Bulls were a tight well-rounded cast who leveraged their strengths. But they did need their superstar to put them over the top.

The true brilliance of the Bulls, then, was coaching. The Bulls had nearly the same supporting cast in 1988 – 1989 under Doug Collins (a fine enough coach — don't get me wrong). In 1990 Phil Jackson took over, but he hadn't yet perfected his 80/20 approach. The Bulls failed 3 years in a row to get past the Detroit Pistons and go on to the finals. The Bulls clearly had the talent, but not the orchestration to leverage that talent. Only the top 20% performed, not the other 80%. The next year of Phil Jackson's leadership of the team, the Bulls beat the Pistons and went on to win the championship. They always had a more talented team than the Pistons. But the Pistons had been far better at leveraging their strengths and minimizing their weaknesses — until Phil Jackson taught the Bulls how to do the same.

Let's look at the Phil Jackson record.

- Phil played on the 1973 NBA championship New York Knicks as a strong role player on a strong team of well-rounded middle 60% players. This team's orchestrated effort easily won the championship (4-1) against a comparably talented, but less well orchestrated, Los Angeles Lakers.

- The same Bulls team that played three years with no championships later won three consecutive NBA championships. The difference? Phil Jackson as head coach orchestrating team efforts and maximizing the middle 60%.

- Here's an example of elevating the Bottom 20%. Jackson created the "Dennis Rodman Emotional Support Group". Before each game, they met to provide emotional compliments to Dennis (and to figuratively "kick his ass"). The result was to turn this Bottom 20% "Hot Head" into a Top 20% defender who proved essential for the team to win.

- Lakers, all the talent in the world — no championship. Add Phil Jackson to orchestrate a well-rounded Middle 60% to maximally leverage the efforts of your top 20% superstars (Shaq and Koby). Result? Three consecutive NBA championships.

- But one year later, when the Lakers top management tied Jackson's hands to let one spoiled superstar have his way and dominate the game? — no championship.

Phil Jackson is no accident! As a Coach he succeeds by pairing and leveraging the Top 20% with a maximized Middle 60% supportive cast, using a minimized Bottom 20% to fill only the most specific niches. The 80/20 Principle exemplified! Let's summarize what we can learn from this instructive (and exciting) period of NBA history. Take a look at the era recap on the following page.

Note: *The Guerilla Teambuilding **(GT)** Approach was described <u>after</u> this time period. I can not (unfortunately) claim credit for the successes listed below. Quite to the contrary, the **(GT)** model was derived — in part — from what I learned by studying this history of success.*

(GT) Approach Success History
NBA Basketball Championships in the Phil Jackson Era

	Team	Coach	Top 20%	Middle 60%	(GT) Used?	Champs?
1989	Bulls	Doug Collins	Jordan, Pipen	Cartwright, Grant, Paxson	No	No
1990	Bulls	Phil Jackson	Jordan, Pipen	Cartwright, Grant, Paxson	No	No
1991	Bulls	Phil Jackson	Jordan, Pipen	Cartwright, Grant, Paxson, others	Yes	Yes
1992	Bulls	Phil Jackson	Jordan, Pipen	Armstrong, Grant, Paxson, others	Yes	Yes
1993	Bulls	Phil Jackson	Jordan, Pipen	Armstrong, Grant, Paxson, others	Yes	Yes
1994	Bulls	Phil Jackson	Pipen	Armstrong, Grant, Kukoc	Yes	No
1995	Bulls	Phil Jackson	Pipen	Armstrong, Kukoc, others	Yes	No
1996	Bulls	Phil Jackson	Jordan, Pipen	Kukoc, Rodman, others	Yes	Yes
1997	Bulls	Phil Jackson	Jordan, Pipen	Kukoc, Rodman, others	Yes	Yes
1998	Bulls	Phil Jackson	Jordan, Pipen	Kukoc, Rodman, others	Yes	Yes
1999	Lakers	Kurt Rambis	Bryant, Shaq	Harper, Rice, others	No	No
2000	Lakers	Phil Jackson	Bryant, Shaq	Harper, Rice, others	Yes	Yes
2001	Lakers	Phil Jackson	Bryant, Shaq	Fox, Grant, others	Yes	Yes
2002	Lakers	Phil Jackson	Bryant, Shaq	Fisher, Fox, others	Yes	Yes
2003	Lakers	Phil Jackson	Bryant, Shaq	Fisher, Fox, others	No	No

Here's what I see.
1. You definitely do need a powerful Top 20%. Without Jordan, no Bulls championship. (1994 — 1995)
2. But superstars aren't enough. You need to use the **(GT)** approach, especially including the 80/20 Principle. (The championship years.)
3. You actually have to *use* the 80/20 Principle. Before Jackson fully developed his 80/20 application (1991) – no championship. When he wasn't allowed to use 80/20 (2003) – no championship.

The first requirement of the **(GT)** model is that you have to use the 80/20 Principle. The rest of this guide will show you how.

Summary Case for (GT)

In closing, the Guerrilla Teambuilding **(GT)** program can help supervisors and managers to improve productivity and satisfaction in the workplace. It provides detailed and systematic approaches that achieve the following.

- **Organize resources for optimal efficiency** and facilitate the work processes of departmental employees (team members).

- **Orchestrate employees' preferences and abilities** in a complementary fashion, maximizing individual and group abilities.

- **Implement leadership strategies** to foster these processes.

- **Optimize peak performance states** which are related to both productivity and satisfaction.

- **Maintain the team practices** created through this model, with ongoing leadership for these Guerrilla Teams.

With the case for adopting **(GT)** well established, let's move on to implementation beginning in **Chapter Three** with the Visual Operations Plan.

Chapter Three

The Visual Operations Plan

Legos

Lego® is a trademark of the Lego Group, and their brilliance is responsible for bringing us this fine product. The Lego, in my opinion, is pure genius — as an organizational system. Many have copied or imitated Lego, but none has duplicated this ingenious application. We all know that Lego builds upon a collection of perfectly interchangeable parts. You can put one here, later move it there, add on as much as your budget will allow. And you never have to worry if the new pieces will fit, if you will have to re-tool, or if they will make these same components five years from now. None of these concerns will ever be a problem. Lego will always work for you! Lego represents interchangeability and standardization in a pure form. I realize that some may see a disheartening aspect here. But I believe this approach will actually enhance, not limit, personal individuality and creativity.

Everyone can see how Legos work for building and manufacturing types of processes. One could use some very big Legos and build a lot of "big stuff." One could also use very small Legos and build a lot of "little stuff" with them. These ideas are not new. Now, think about the organizational systems you see around you. No doubt you see numerous aspects of this basic concept in your own office. For example, the entire franchising industry is built on these concepts (not necessarily the most appealing application of these ideas, but very effective). The movement to standardize and interchange on mass scales has been underway for a long time. We see it all around us, every day. I still contend that no one has captured the concept quite as well as the standard "6-prong" Lego.

This basic *standardization* model fits very nicely, and very effectively, into the structure of workgroups and organizations. As part of the selection team for initial employees at the Diamond Star Motors Plant [ii], I learned that Japanese manufacturing teams are fairly advanced in their use of these ideas. The Mitsubishi group emphasized cross-training in tasks, continuous performance and safety improvement discussions, as well as very high degrees of flexibility, interchangeability and uniformity.

Kaizen

These topics were all subsumed under the general umbrella of "Kaizen" for the Mitsubishi team. There were real lessons to learn from these executives, and my participation was a great opportunity to study their methods (and a wonderful experience).

The reader would do well to investigate the Kaizen® Institute web site found in the resources section of this guide for additional information on this topic (KAIZEN and GEMBAKAIZEN are trademarks of KAIZEN Institute, Ltd.). This subject's focus on standardization, interchangeability, and the importance of team discussion and planning contributes significantly towards understanding the foundations of the **(GT)** program. As such, a brief review and clarification of the topic is presented in **Appendix D** (page 119), and additional source material is cited there and in **References** (page 124). The Kaizen discussion process can do wonders for improving efficiency and creating seamless interfaces within an organization. My experiences at the Diamond Star Assessment Center created my belief that a highly productive and efficient organizational structure can be formed if key interfaces can become as easy as snapping Legos together.

Key Considerations of the Visual Operations Plan

Following are some key considerations when undertaking such an organizational makeover.

- **"Parts is Parts".** Every organization and / or workgroup is capable of breaking its service and product lines into component parts that assemble together to uniquely meet the needs of clients.

- **Know the Map to Navigate.** The effectiveness of each team member depends on their knowledge of this plan and how to navigate this system.

- **Know Your Services Like the Back of Your Hand.** To be a truly effective Guerrilla Team, this plan must be the foundation of all interactions, role assignments and effectiveness appraisals.

- **Quick and Dirty.** The **(GT)** Visual Operations Plan approach is a powerful, quick reference model through which all team members can instantly comprehend how to navigate the organizational system efficiently and effectively.

- **Words are Not Enough.** The simple existence of a written plan to address these issues does not ensure immediacy of recall and internalization of the concepts for a team or workgroup.

- **Written Plans Do Not Equal Action.** The existence of a written plan or system does not automatically imbue team members with the skill to apply the plan to their work processes.

- **Visual is Better.** A system must be clear, simple, direct — preferably, *visual*, to promote this immediacy of recall and internalization of content.

Visual Operations Plan Tools

The remainder of **Chapter Three** presents the tools you will use to institute this approach in your own organization.

- **Visual Operations Plan Foundation.** A narrative example of an organizational process (in the behavioral health arena) for creating building-blocks and *standardization* is provided.

- **Visual Operations Plan Examples.** Visual Operations Plan*s* for a variety of knowledge-based, service-related organizations illustrate this application, and can be found in Figures 1 — 6 (found at the end of the chapter, pp. 25 — 30).

- **Visual Operations Plan Exercise.** An exercise designed to be used as a general template for the production of a Visual Operations Plan (Figures 7 A through C) is found at the end of **Chapter Three** as well (pp. 31 — 33).

Applying these tools to your own organization will define *your* Building-Blocks. These building-blocks, similar to Lego, can be snapped on and off to create a specific service package for *your* clients and / or internal operations referrals.

Visual Operations Plan Foundation

The Visual Operations Plan is an extremely versatile organizational model. It is effective across most work areas that require coordinated efforts. I happen to be a clinical psychologist by training, and many of my uses of this approach have been in the behavioral health arena. The foundational example presented here is a behavioral health implementation of this process.

Providing child and adolescent behavioral healthcare is a unique undertaking. To service moderate-to-severe cases requires a team of highly trained and dedicated professionals comprising many different disciplines and educational levels. Care providers must perform a number of steps, including an initial assessment, service access provision, coordination of care across many service providers and the monitoring of progress and outcomes. This is no small task. My experience has shown that every step of this process must compatibly build upon the previous one, or outcomes may be unsuccessful. The negative results can include confused and irritated families, unproductive and damaging in-fighting amongst staff and professionals, and unorchestrated and ineffective overall care.

But, it doesn't have to be that way. Proper organization and coordination of team resources always results in improved care provision. Although the particular product may vary greatly, just about any business system carries out a similar array of functions. As a manager for many such service delivery systems, I have found the following approaches to be successful.

When I initially assessed the process flow for the child & adolescent behavioral healthcare team, it was clear that we could begin improvements right at the beginning of the process. When a family presents with a concern, the behavioral health team assesses family needs by taking a history and inventory of current difficulties. This task is intended to tailor a care package to that family. In the system I evaluated, several professionals participated in this initial assessment. For example, psychologists conducted psychological assessments, psychiatrists evaluated medication management issues and case managers conducted needs assessments. Each would gather similar pieces of information.

Our team's first *standardizing* systemic intervention created an initial assessment procedure to greatly reduce repetition. Some professionals might have the need to gather specialized information, but no longer would the same information be collected over and over. This required a great deal of compromise, goodwill, and trust among the staff. Each discipline had to trust and accept that all assessments included a core set of information, gathered upfront in the process. And all disciplines had to agree on the content of this core set of information. To establish the goodwill and trust necessary to make this improvement work required teambuilding. I will explain more about the process as our discussion continues.

Next, our team realized that our various services had to "fit" together better. We had to break down the traditional "departmental" barriers and offer a tightly-meshed array of services that made logical sense to both the clients and the staff. This required the creation of basic "building-blocks." First and foremost, every client needed one primary and basic component of care: a therapist. If other services were inadequate or unavailable, this person would remain the client's "rock," source of information, advocate, and primary helper. There are obvious analogous roles in other customer-oriented business applications.

On this base "building-block," other services could be added as warranted. For instance, if a child experienced difficulties getting along with others at school or in the community, the team could "snap-on" someone whose job it was to go help the child on-site. (In our system, these professionals are called case managers.) If a parent needed help inside the home to better manage a child's misbehavior, we could "snap-on" the same type of intervention within the home setting. If we wanted to be able to create success for the child in a group setting with other children, we could "create" successful experiences with the "snap-on" of a socialization group[iii]. If the child was capable of talking through certain issues with other children, we might "snap-on" a processing group in which the child could address specific issues. Some children get into serious trouble at home or in the community by showing aggression, extreme emotional reactions or highly destructive behaviors. For these children, the team could "snap-on" a structured, socially-based after-school program for 1 to 5 days a week.

The base building-block, the therapist, had the ability to "snap-on" these other building-block interventions as needed. There were often multiple concurrent referral building-blocks of professional opinions that contributed suggestions for additional resources. An in-depth psychological assessment – itself a building-block – might discern a requirement for a behavioral therapy building-block. A psychiatric evaluation – also a building block – might recommend a medication intervention building-block. All the building-blocks, in their various shapes and colors, were available for the primary caregiver to "snap-on" — and off — to build a tailored treatment structure for client families.

To make these services even more accessible, we added the option to client families' to walk in from 9am to 7pm, eliminating the need for initial appointments. If that didn't work, the option of going to the client's home, if needed, to start the process was also added. Now that's a user-friendly behavioral health system!

With this new approach, there is minimal duplication of effort and paperwork. There is minimal service overlap, and the client family receives much more extensive services than any one professional could provide. When a child is "driving you crazy" — as parents would often describe — the family does not want to run around town getting a building-block here and another there, from a dozen different service providers. This is especially burdensome when the family is not even sure which building-block(s) they or their child needs. Such parents want to go to one place where they are treated nicely, where they can see all the various pieces on-site, where they can see their provider "make" their intervention plan and where their life is improved.

After 20 years in the field of behavioral health, I can say that a litany of "I cant's" is unfortunately an all-too-common response to consumers. The system presented here, along with its comprehensive offerings, is rare. Figures 1 and 2 (pp. 25 — 26) illustrate this behavioral health system example. They display the component building-blocks of the system and some examples of how individualized service plans could combine these.

Visual Operations Plan Examples

The adolescent behavioral healthcare scenario presented above and in Figures 1 and 2 is one example of how to develop a Visual Operations Plan. Hopefully, you are already thinking about how this approach might benefit your organization. To further stimulate your thinking, this **(GT)** guide includes more examples, some exercises, and an Implementation Checklist. Following are suggestions for how you should utilize these materials.

- **Figures 1 and 2** (pp. 25 — 26) illustrate the *behavioral health* system presented in the example. They display the component building-blocks of the system, the overall **Visual Operations Plan**, and some examples of how these could be combined in individualized service plans.

- **To allow for comparison and contrast** to other service delivery systems, Figures 3 through 6 (pp. 27 — 30) illustrate how this same model might be used in **Visual Operations Plans** across other specific sectors.

- **Figures 7 A through C** (pp. 31 — 33) provide exercises that can be used to create **Visual Operations Plans** for your specific work setting and to develop individualized service delivery plans comprised of your own building-blocks that address specific client needs, be they "internal" or "external" clients.

- Finally, the first Implementation Checklist is provided at the end of **Chapter Three** (page 34). This should be used to stimulate team discussion, as the first step toward implementing **(GT)** within your organization.

Figure 1

Visual Operations Plan example

Behavioral Health Service Delivery Model

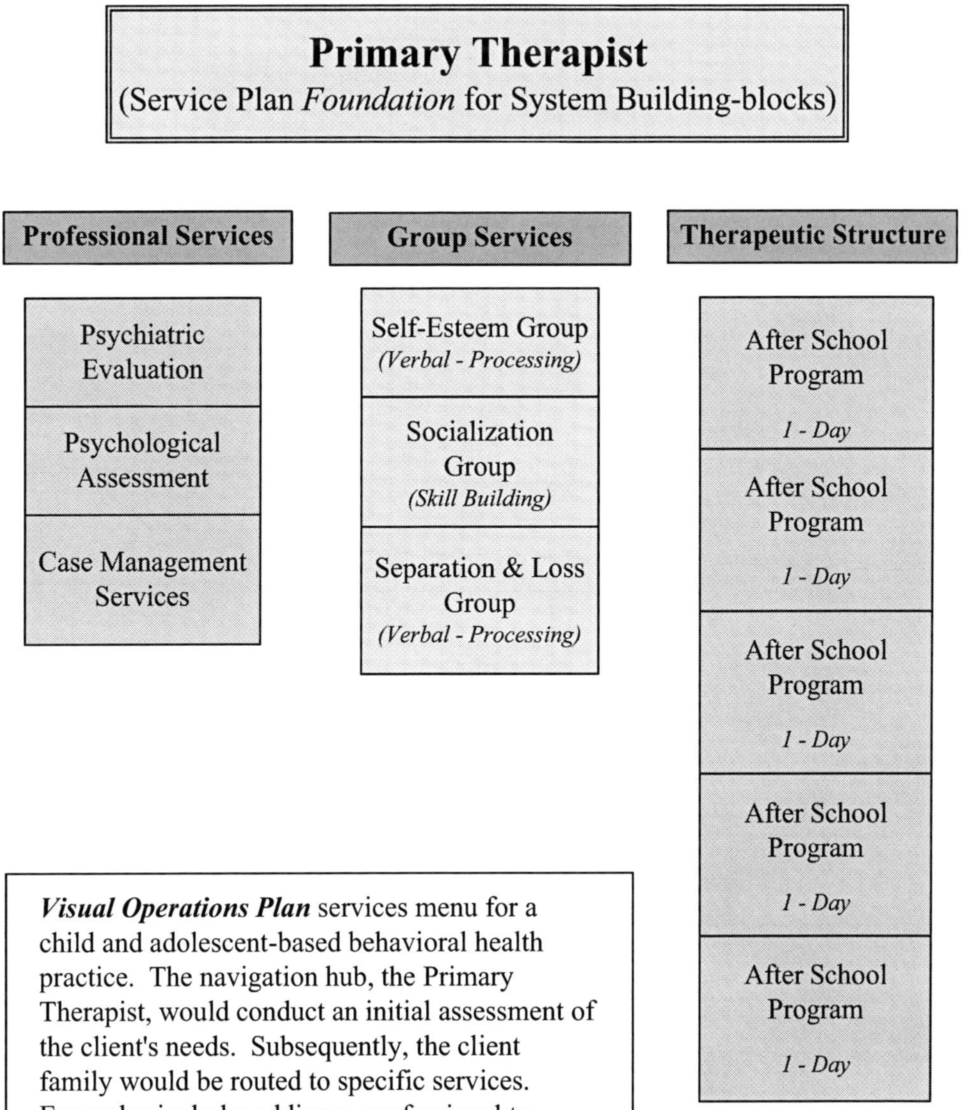

Primary Therapist
(Service Plan *Foundation* for System Building-blocks)

Professional Services	Group Services	Therapeutic Structure
Psychiatric Evaluation	Self-Esteem Group *(Verbal - Processing)*	After School Program *1 - Day*
Psychological Assessment	Socialization Group *(Skill Building)*	After School Program *1 - Day*
Case Management Services	Separation & Loss Group *(Verbal - Processing)*	After School Program *1 - Day*
		After School Program *1 - Day*
		After School Program *1 - Day*

Visual Operations Plan services menu for a child and adolescent-based behavioral health practice. The navigation hub, the Primary Therapist, would conduct an initial assessment of the client's needs. Subsequently, the client family would be routed to specific services. Examples include: adding a professional to monitor the case, adding therapy groups of several types, and adding structured time to a client's day. The Primary Therapist remains the overall service delivery coordinator.

Figure 2

Visual Operations Plan example

Behavioral Health Service Building Blocks

Building-blocks are selected based upon family service needs assessment.

Presenting Problems

- The child is notably depressed because of parental divorce.

- This depression has notably interfered with school performance.

- The depression has unusual symptom severity and onset features.

- The child is worried that peers will not accept the changes in her family.

Intervention (Building-block) Plan

- A Primary Therapist is assigned to provide therapy and schedule access to additional services.

- A Case Manager is assigned to assist at school and coordinate with teaching staff.

- A Psychological Assessment is performed to clarify diagnosis and the features of depression.

- Separation & Loss group participation is initiated to normalize family change experience and provide support.

Visual Operations Plan services

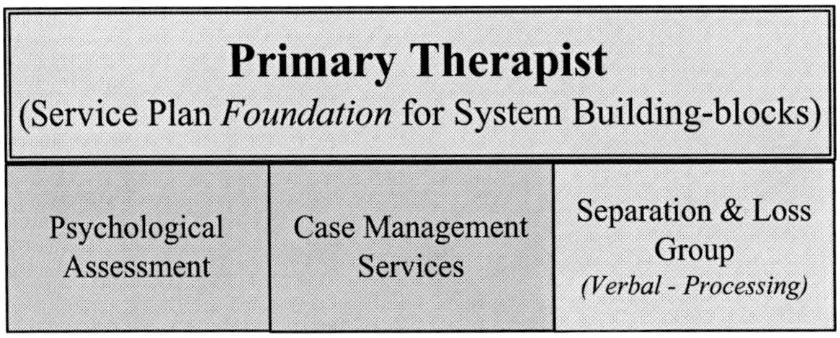

Primary Therapist		
(Service Plan *Foundation* for System Building-blocks)		
Psychological Assessment	Case Management Services	Separation & Loss Group *(Verbal - Processing)*

Figure 3

Visual Operations Plan example

Medical Service Delivery Model

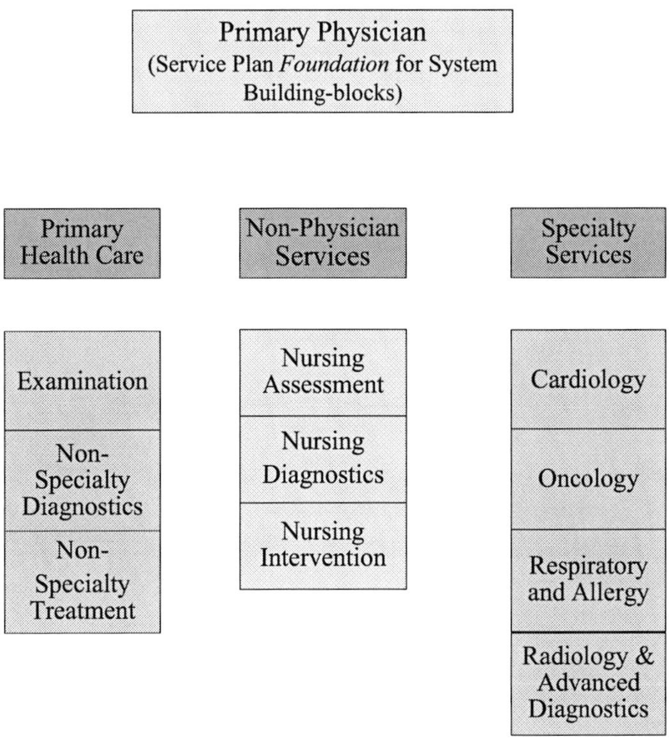

Primary Physician
(Service Plan *Foundation* for System Building-blocks)

Primary Health Care	Non-Physician Services	Specialty Services

Examination	Nursing Assessment	Cardiology
Non-Specialty Diagnostics	Nursing Diagnostics	Oncology
Non-Specialty Treatment	Nursing Intervention	Respiratory and Allergy
		Radiology & Advanced Diagnostics

Visual Operations Plan services menu for a medical practice. The navigation hub, the Primary Physician, would conduct an initial assessment of the patient's needs. Subsequently, the patient would be routed to desired services. Examples include routine diagnostic tests, interventions, a specializing professional or multiple service areas. The Primary Physician remains the overall service delivery coordinator.

Figure 4

Visual Operations Plan example

Legal Services Delivery Model

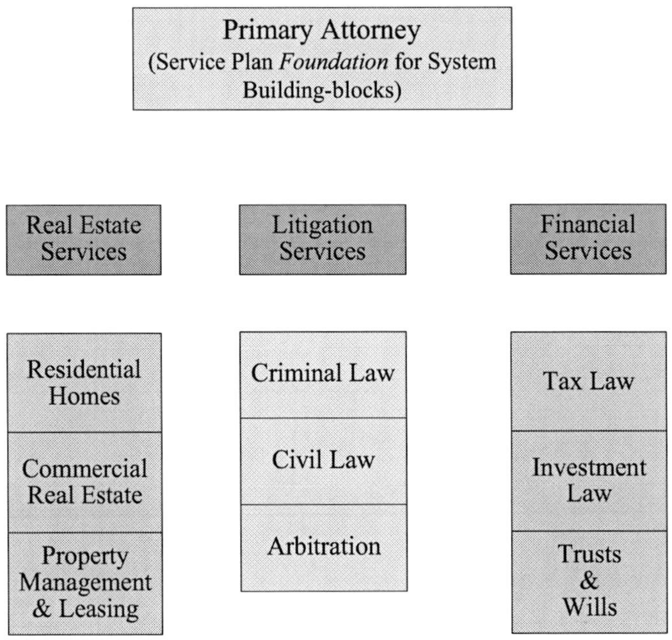

Primary Attorney
(Service Plan *Foundation* for System Building-blocks)

Real Estate Services	Litigation Services	Financial Services

Residential Homes	Criminal Law	Tax Law
Commercial Real Estate	Civil Law	Investment Law
Property Management & Leasing	Arbitration	Trusts & Wills

Visual Operations Plan services menu for a legal practice. The navigation hub, the Primary Attorney, would conduct an initial assessment of the client's needs. The client would then be routed to specializing professional(s) in the desired area(s) that can best address presenting legal concerns. Of course, various professionals with differing areas of expertise can create a specialized legal services team.

Figure 5

Visual Operations Plan example

Real Estate Brokerage Service Delivery Model

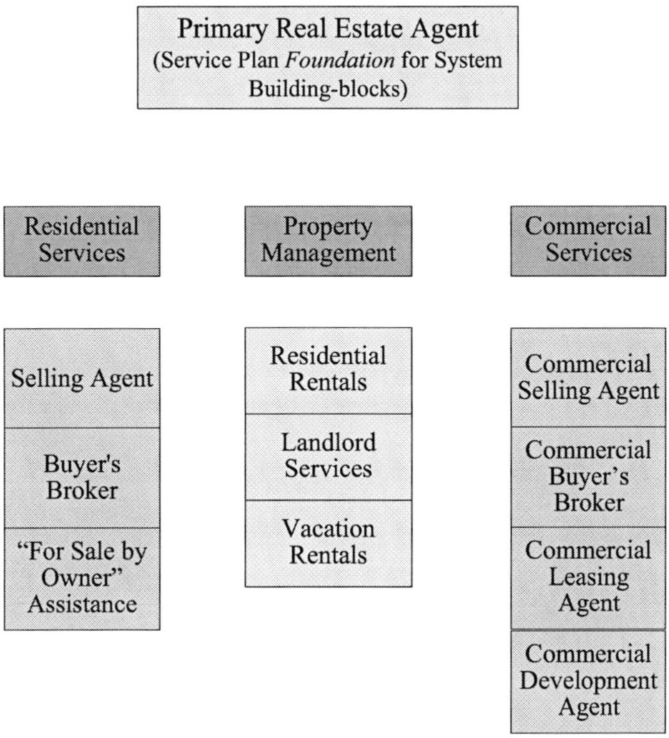

Primary Real Estate Agent
(Service Plan *Foundation* for System Building-blocks)

Residential Services	Property Management	Commercial Services

Selling Agent	Residential Rentals	Commercial Selling Agent
Buyer's Broker	Landlord Services	Commercial Buyer's Broker
"For Sale by Owner" Assistance	Vacation Rentals	Commercial Leasing Agent
		Commercial Development Agent

Visual Operations Plan services menu for Real Estate services. The navigation hub, the Primary Agent, would conduct an initial assessment and route a client to specializing professional(s) in the desired area of expertise, based upon presenting client needs.

Figure 6

Visual Operations Plan example

Lending Institution Delivery Model

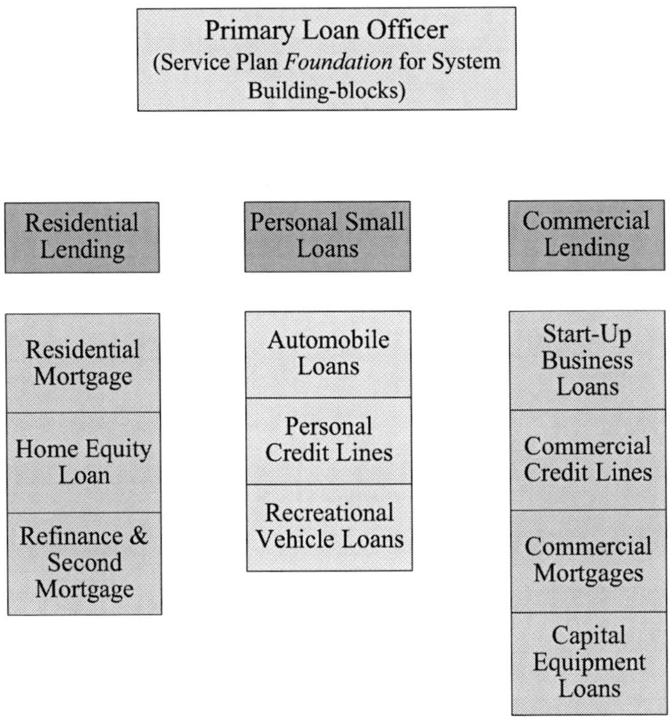

```
              ┌─────────────────────────────┐
              │   Primary Loan Officer       │
              │ (Service Plan Foundation for System │
              │      Building-blocks)        │
              └─────────────────────────────┘


  ┌──────────────┐   ┌──────────────┐   ┌──────────────┐
  │ Residential  │   │Personal Small│   │  Commercial  │
  │   Lending    │   │    Loans     │   │   Lending    │
  └──────────────┘   └──────────────┘   └──────────────┘

  ┌──────────────┐   ┌──────────────┐   ┌──────────────┐
  │ Residential  │   │  Automobile  │   │   Start-Up   │
  │  Mortgage    │   │    Loans     │   │   Business   │
  │              │   │              │   │    Loans     │
  ├──────────────┤   ├──────────────┤   ├──────────────┤
  │ Home Equity  │   │  Personal    │   │  Commercial  │
  │    Loan      │   │ Credit Lines │   │ Credit Lines │
  │              │   ├──────────────┤   │              │
  ├──────────────┤   │ Recreational │   ├──────────────┤
  │ Refinance &  │   │Vehicle Loans │   │  Commercial  │
  │   Second     │   │              │   │  Mortgages   │
  │  Mortgage    │   └──────────────┘   │              │
  └──────────────┘                      ├──────────────┤
                                        │   Capital    │
                                        │  Equipment   │
                                        │    Loans     │
                                        └──────────────┘
```

┌───┐
│ *Visual Operations Plan* services menu for │
│ financial lending products. The navigation │
│ hub, the Primary Loan Officer, assists a │
│ client to access the services / products within │
│ the system.   │
└───┘

Figure 7A

Visual Operations Plan example

Component Pieces Template Exercise

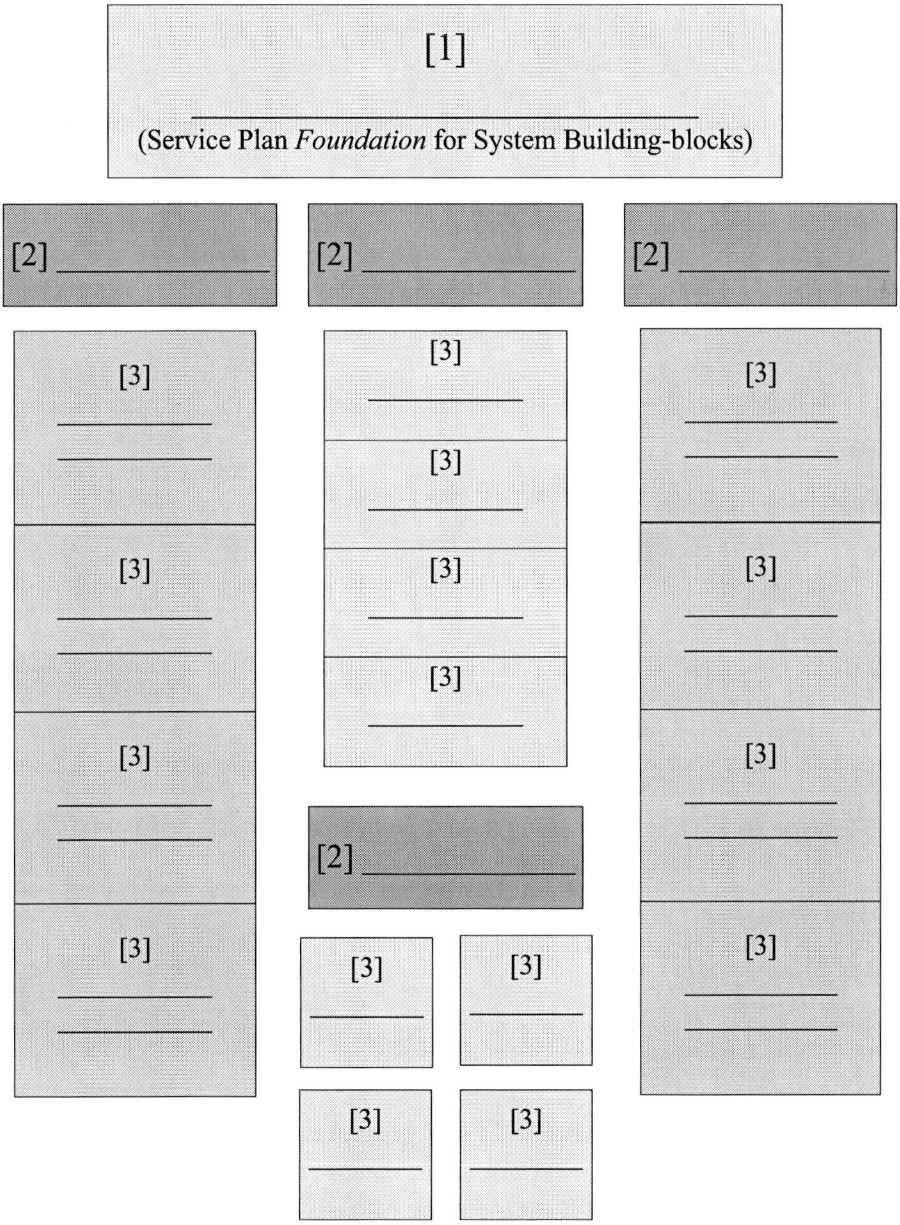

[1]

(Service Plan *Foundation* for System Building-blocks)

[2] _____

[2] _____

[2] _____

[3]

_____

_____

[3]

_____

_____

[3]

_____

_____

[3]

_____

_____

[3]

_____

[3]

_____

[3]

_____

[3]

_____

[2] _____

[3]

_____

_____

[3]

_____

_____

[3]

_____

_____

[3]

_____

_____

[3]

_____

[3]

_____

[3]

_____

[3]

_____

Figure 7B

Visual Operations Plan example

Instructions for Component Pieces Template Exercise

[1]

_____

(Service Plan *Foundation* for System Building-blocks)

In area [1] on *Figure 7(A)*, identify the designated position, tool, or service your organization will use (or currently uses) as a foundation or basis from which services and / or products can be accessed by customers (internal or external). This role, position, or Foundation will organize and / or hold all other **Building-blocks** (services – products) for this order or customer. This Foundation is the key navigation hub for your system.

[2] _____

In area [2] on *Figure 7(A)*, identify a type of service or product line that clients will want to access. This will serve as a general organizational heading for several specific component **Building-blocks**.

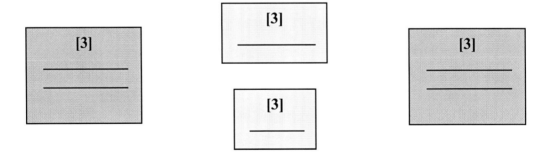

In area [3] on *Figure 7(A)*, identify the component **Building-blocks**. These are specific services or products that organizational team members must access or obtain for customers. Combine the component **Building-blocks** into unique structures that will address specific client requests

Figure 7C

Visual Operations Plan Exercise

Service Delivery Planning Exercise

(1) **Service Area:** _____

(2) **Presenting Client Needs:** _____

_____

_____

(3) **Service Plan**: _____

_____

_____

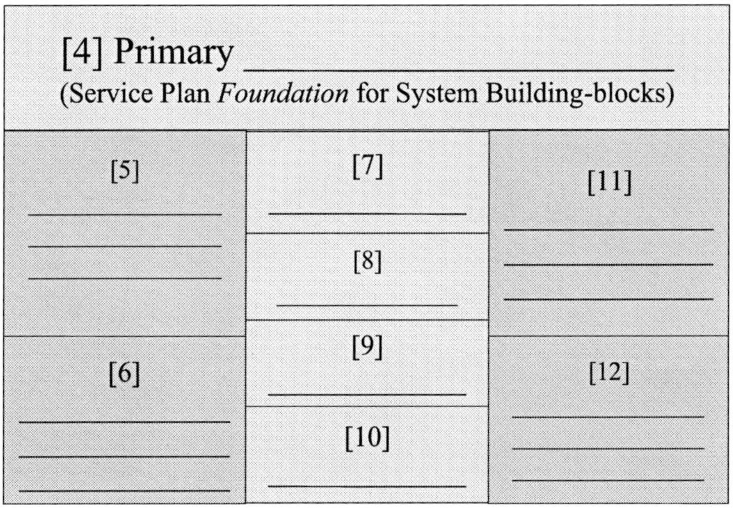

<table>
<tr><td colspan="3">[4] Primary _____
(Service Plan Foundation for System Building-blocks)</td></tr>
<tr><td>[5]
_____
_____
_____</td><td>[7]
_____
[8]
_____</td><td>[11]
_____
_____</td></tr>
<tr><td>[6]
_____
_____</td><td>[9]
_____
[10]
_____</td><td>[12]
_____
_____</td></tr>
</table>

In Area (1):   *Define* the service your organization provides.

In Area (2):   *Identify* the needs your client has for seeking your services.

In Area (3):   *Match* the ***Visual Operations*** services / products you will link with the clients, and help them navigate, to satisfy their service request needs.

In Area (4):   *Name* the primary mechanism or person (***Foundation***) through which the client will access and navigate these services.

In Areas (5 through 12):   *Label* the individual building-blocks that will be accessed to meet the client's service request needs within the service delivery plan (use only the building-blocks needed from exercise 7A).

Implementation Checklist 1

The Visual Operations Plan

- What are the steps, processes, and services required to create, package, and fulfill your organization's output demands for delivery to customers or clients?

- How do these steps and processes fit together?

- What are the strengths in your organization's integration of these processes?

- What are the weaknesses in integration?

- What ideas can team members suggest for how to improve this integration (remember Kaizen)?

- How can technology play a role to improve this integration?

- What are the basic building-blocks you want to create or restructure to make your systems more *standardized*? How can these basic building-blocks best fit together in a "snap-on / snap-off" manner?

<u>Notes:</u>

Chapter Four

Team Structure and Communication
The "Proximity" Model & The "Meet = Do" Model

Face-to-Face Meetings

Effective teams have to meet and must have effective post-meeting communication. I emphasize that there is no substitute for face-to-face meetings because only these can fulfill the following key functions.

1. **Building a sense of team:**

    *   **You are not friends with someone unless** you physically do things together. The same applies to teams. Teams <u>do</u> things together.

    *   **To be part of something larger,** people have to meet. Team members might share disparate pieces of work, or a project, but they are not a team unless they meet.

    *   **Could you teleconference?** You could, but the key here is the feeling of unity. You should only teleconference if you can do so in a way that engenders this sense of unity. You *must* create this feeling.

    *   **There must be some face-to-face.** There are no effective substitutes for direct meetings. Even if these meetings are only periodic, people need "face time".

    *   **Other forms of meeting** can be effective once a strong team has emerged. But not when initially creating that sense of team — not a Guerrilla Team anyway!

2. **Accomplishing a task:**

    *   **Assembly line.** Think of your team meeting as a small assembly line.

    *   **While you have all these key people together,** maximize the opportunity. You will not often be together outside of this meeting room, so use the time to *make something*!

    *   **All assembly lines make things.** Parts go in, a product comes out. The fewer steps you have in the process, the more efficient it will be.

    *   **Do something!** Don't just talk about it! You will then have eliminated at least one additional step.

    *   **Knowledge = Parts.** Your parts in this assembly line are the knowledge and expertise of the team members.

- **The final product of your meeting** may be a document or a completed form. If you work in a creative industry, you may create an ad, a dress, a design. If you are an engineering team, your meeting might result in an actual widget. Your product may be only a prototype widget, but a widget nonetheless.

- **Tap into the ideas *right-then-and-there*, and immediately implement them. Do not go your separate ways and wait an hour, or a day, or even a week to <u>do</u> something.

3. Building a sense of common function (*esprit de corps*):

- **Not only do the team members meet physically**, but when they meet, they also accomplish things! This tangible, commonly developed work result serves as a physical token of teamwork.

- **Meeting becomes a way that things get done and not a drudgery.** For example, if I have to depend on Maria, Jane or Jim to get things done, I can see things accomplished right in front of me. This lessens the logistical difficulties of repeatedly seeking out these people. It gives me increased confidence in them, because I actually see the results of their work tangibly, directly, and immediately.

- **Interconnected function.** A basic premise of the Guerrilla Teambuilding **(GT)** model is that teams are exponentially more effective when they display this interconnected function.

- **Common function = Unification.** You are not only more efficient when you accomplish tasks directly in meetings, but you also have a much more unified and stronger team as a result!

4. Tie it all together

- Make your meeting agenda a *living* document that members can add to while they are working individually, or with pairings or subgroups (remember the *80/20 pairing guidelines*, and *80/20 hoop dreams*!).

- Schedule all your sub-group meetings prior to departure from the larger GT meeting. Why not make these part of the agenda or *living document*.

- Simply fill in the blanks in the sub-groupings or individual work areas of the *living document* and bring back to the larger GT for assembly of all the component pieces (*snap-on, snap-off*).

- Keep in touch with team members and key pairings with special ongoing arrangements such as email sub-groupings, IM's, blackberry connections. Try to maintain open, quick ongoing communication and access.

- Illustration 1 (on the following page) highlights this post-meeting communication process.

Illustration 1

The Post Meeting Communication Process

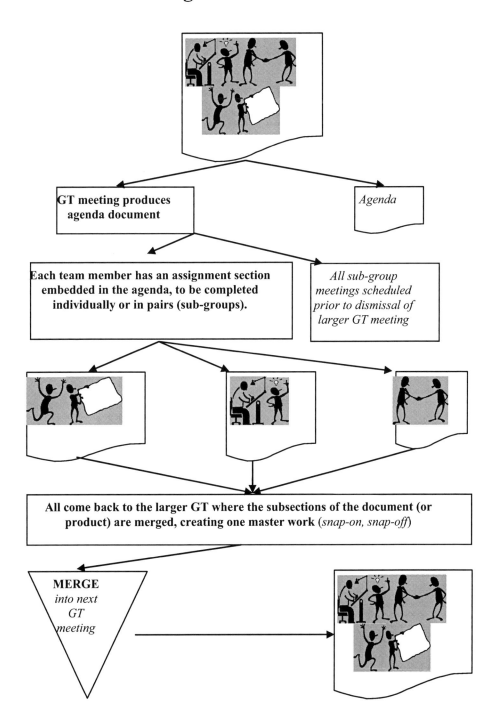

Team Meeting Forms

To further explore meeting concepts, the following pages present a continuum — or hierarchy — of team meeting forms. They are presented in order from the least effective meeting form to most effective meeting form. Undoubtedly, you will recognize these examples. Almost everyone has taken part in these types of meetings at one time or another.

Illustration 2

The informal meeting

- Information exchanged

- Relationships enhanced

- Functionality on a hit or miss basis

- Little accomplished

A. **Teams get together informally to *rap.***

- **This is all well and good**, and may indeed be a necessary component of teambuilding. But, in and of itself, it is simply not a sufficient reason to meet or an effective means of achieving goals.

- **It can also become a very unproductive habit** if done excessively or if it serves as the only form of meeting structure within a group or team.

- **If channeled in a negative direction**, frequent informal *rap* time, in the absence of other formal meeting structures, can become destructive to ultimate goal achievement.

Illustration 3

The "bitch" session

- Unproductive – in fact, counter-productive
- Repetitive

B. Team members get together for what is intended to be a formal meeting and spend their time complaining.

- This is not good.

- **Ultimate distraction.** The meeting, while possibly being viewed as supportive, and maybe even enjoyable, distracts from the ultimate focus.

- **"Why do I have to do this"?** The meeting then becomes viewed as a non-essential adjunct to the job and subsequently as something that people would like to avoid or begin to complain about attending.

- **When discussion does not equal action.** It can also take on an inappropriately negative tone (similar to the issues presented in structure A) and / or get people into the mindset that group discussion and action are not connected.

- This is ultimately counterproductive.

Illustration 4

The scheduled meeting

- Functional coordination of efforts

- Delayed results

- Limited feedback loops increase revision times

C. **Teams meet and engage in actual problem solving and then** *GO THEIR SEPARATE WAYS TO IMPLEMENT STRATEGIES.*

- **This is better.** But it still is not the most effective level of organization.

- **Memory and steps.** There are too many things to remember, and too many steps and too many points where something can go awry. Follow-up may be hampered by needing direct expertise of team members.

- **Back and forth.** You also lose the direct feedback of the group. This will increase time spent in the revision process. It is inevitable that someone will object to individual efforts when these are brought back to the group.

- **Remember OHIO — Only Handle It Once!** This repetition of efforts — inherent in many revision processes - is ultimately an OHIO violation that greatly slows progress.

- **This may not destroy** *Flow* **(peak performance),** but it certainly does not enhance it. (**Chapter Six** addresses the OHIO and *Flow* models.)

Illustration 5

The Guerrilla Team Meeting Structure

- Formal and informal meeting time geared around goal accomplishment
- Work is accomplished with all key parties present

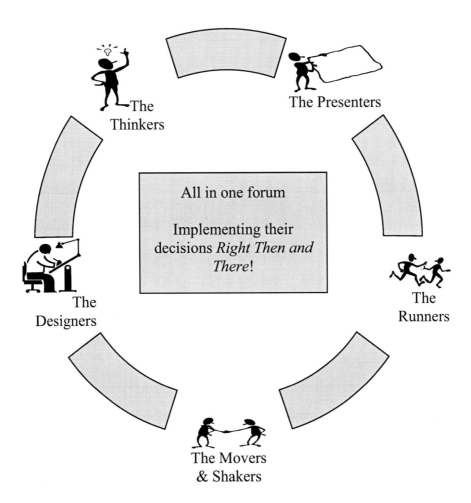

D. The best strategy

- **Continuous blocks of time:** Teams meet for extended blocks of time.

- **Within these blocks** of time, there is an obvious proximity and social component; there is a structure to ensure task accomplishment; there is an actual product created in the meeting — not just talked about; and there is an *esprit de corps* of people working together.

- **Implement the plan.** If the team is going to talk about a plan in a meeting, why not take the next steps to implement the plan *right-then-and-there*?

- **Create the document.** If the team must talk about information to create a document, then why not create the document *right-then-and-there*?

- **Make the Widget.** If the team is commissioned to create something, even if it needs to be finished later, then why not make it, or start the process, *right-then-and-there*?

- *Right-then-and-there* **greatly reduces communication problems**, phone tag, and some weaknesses of design by committee within a standard revision process.

- **Maximizing strengths.** By utilizing this meeting structure, you maximize the strengths of the team, you minimize the weaknesses of individuals, you get a lot more accomplished and you greatly reduce the *drudgery* of tasks by accomplishing them *right-then-and-there*.

- **Peak performance.** You also create a great *Flow* as a result of this process, as well as a sense of camaraderie and unification.

- **The way we get things done.** People begin to view meetings as "the way we get things done" and not as a hindrance to the end goal or as a minor step in the process.

Improving team meeting effectiveness is an action that can be taken *right now*. And the technique is easy. Whenever you, as the team manager or group supervisor, call a meeting – Declare Your Outcome. Ideally, the meeting title (i.e., subject line) should name the document, design, product or other outcome to be produced. Always identify a specific *physical deliverable* that will be the outcome or product of the meeting. Ensure that all team members necessary to produce a result will be present at the meeting.

At the outset of the meeting, Declare Your Outcome. At first, you may have to steer wandering discussion back to this outcome (perhaps, repeatedly). After a while, however, don't be surprised if your team members begin steering for you. Tangible outcomes are a powerful source of immediate gratification. Your team will naturally strive to attain these.

Don't allow the meeting to conclude without a *physical deliverable*. Even if it's a rough first draft, don't disband until you can hold up in the air the tangible result of your team effort. In fact, do exactly that as a way to end the meeting!

An initiation and implementation of these practices follows in **Team Structure**. It continues using the behavioral health example presented in the previous chapter. The example allows you to view this meeting structure issue within an application area likely differing from your organization's, but provides you with an exercise in generalizing and applying this process within your own work environment.

Team Structure

Here is another behavioral health example to illustrate implementation of this new approach to meeting.

Behavioral health (indeed, all of healthcare), like many industries, requires a great deal of paperwork and documentation. When I joined my current agency, I was overwhelmed by the amount of paper I had to complete — and by the drudgery of doing it! I wasn't alone with this feeling. All of the direct care staff hated our paperwork. We would get together to complain about our paperwork and, consequently, not get our paperwork done! Our management would hound us about not doing our paperwork. We, in response, would meet to complain about management, and still not get our paperwork done. Committees formed to reduce the amount of paperwork, but they never really accomplished much. The paper kept flowing and, worse yet, it kept changing. The whole cycle of hating the task, complaining about the task, not completing the task, getting in trouble for not completing the task, and complaining about the trouble we were in, was out of control. I had to devise a way out — for my own sanity.

Midway into my first year at this clinic, I had been part of another team and found it an exciting endeavor. We talked about cases, attempted to coordinate our efforts, and made real problem-solving plans. The whole experience would have been great except for the fact that when these highly rewarding team meetings were over, I still had to go back and do all my paperwork independently — while isolated in my office. And now I had less time to do it, because I spent more of my time in team meetings. This still wasn't accomplishing my goals of streamlining the paperwork drudgery!

As the new guy, one of my paperwork chores was to write all the psychological reports. To address this report-writing challenge, I approached my supervisor (a very nice, sincere, and experienced senior psychologist) with a proposal. He said I could give my approach a try. At the next team meeting, with all members present, I set out to question everybody, review test results, and write down our feedback. I hoped to have a finished report at the end of the meeting. I thought it was a great idea, but in this particular case, it really wasn't.

My supervisor soon felt the meeting no longer accomplished his goals. Because of our opposing goals, we could not keep the meeting focused. The other staff members became confused, and we had to scrap the format. In retrospect, I handled this initiation process poorly. I failed to prepare the team members for this change, and I didn't structure the meeting to accomplish common goals. It should have been a win-win situation, but it was not. The experience did, however, leave me with the belief that the process could be highly effective, if handled the right way.

Because I was very vocal, innovative (if I may say so), and — most importantly — productive (i.e., I brought in a lot of money for the agency), I was given an opportunity to recruit people who wanted to work on a new type of clinical team. On this team, we would share all our clients (usually very needy families who required multiple and simultaneous services). We would meet for 4-6 hours/week. In our meetings we would complete our required client paperwork together, and we would create the documents and reports we needed – *right-then-and-there*.

Prior to this endeavor, our clinic functioned as a group of independent practitioners. We would periodically discuss some of our cases with each other, and occasionally make a referral to a specialty service. This was effective for some clinical areas. But for most Child and Adolescent (C&A) therapy cases, it was grossly ineffective. Practitioners were frustrated, managing very difficult families who needed multiple services. But as individual practitioners they had no ready access to these services, or a means to monitor care effectively.

To my surprise, I had many volunteers for the new Child and Adolescent clinical team. And when we started our new team process, we caught on *fire*!

If we had stopped with collectively doing our paperwork within a staffing-based model, that would have been a significant accomplishment by itself. But we took the team process a step further. We coordinated all client care through these team meetings, establishing our clinical plans and implementing what we could – *right-then-and-there.* We greatly reduced the drudgery of paperwork, and actually made it enjoyable and rewarding through a team discussion format. We utilized our collective strengths and abilities to coordinate care to a new level that was well beyond what we could accomplish individually. Team members relished team meeting times. The new meeting structure accomplished all the productivity goals and team-building aspects hoped for, and then some. We had figuratively *built a better mouse trap*.

The processes utilized here will create successful team meetings in nearly any setting. These team meetings are an indispensable tool for goal completion. Now that you have an example of pulling together the meeting structure task, give it a try. The second Implementation Checklist is provided on the next page to help you with this task, and should be used as a basis for team discussion, as the next step toward implementing **(GT)** within your organization.

Implementation Checklist 2

Team Structure

- What style do your current team meetings resemble?

- What do you do in team meetings?

- How are these team meetings structured?

- How do people feel about team meetings?

- Do people complain about team meetings?

- Do people avoid team meetings?

- Are team meetings tantamount to complaint sessions?

- Do team meetings take on a problem-solving tone?

- Do team meetings assign specific tasks accomplished outside the meeting?

- Do team meetings involve planning and actual implementation within the team meeting?

- Do team meetings involve the accomplishment of tasks viewed as drudgery or highly difficult individual assignments?

- Do team meetings lessen the workload of the individuals who attend the meetings?

- Do team meetings represent the "way things get done" versus an aside to this process?

- Do team meetings produce a sense of camaraderie and / or *esprit de corps*?

- How could restructured team meetings accomplish these latter objectives, that is, promoting task accomplishment, alleviating drudgery and encouraging *esprit de corps*?

Notes:

Chapter Five

Know the Team — Know the Coach

Guerilla Teambuilding **(GT)** is all about optimizing your most valuable resources – the team members themselves. The goals are to facilitate team work processes and enable the leveraged application of the full collective strengths of the entire team. The process for achieving these goals is to artfully combine and focus the skills and capabilities of all team members for maximum effectiveness.

In order to do that, you must thoroughly understand your resources – who they are. You need to *know* your team. And, remember that the team leader is a critical member of the team. It's best to start at the top and *know* the coach.

Knowing may seem to be an imprecise goal. Luckily, a structured mechanism with long-established validity for providing this insight is readily available, and cost-effective to use.

This chapter of Guerilla Teambuilding **(GT)** will guide you through this critical *knowing* process. A lot of material is presented, so here's an outline.

- First, I'll discuss the general concepts and considerations of **The Interpersonal Insight Process**.

- With this conceptual foundation, I'll describe the recommended tools for conducting the *knowing* process, in a sub-section titled **Overview for the Use of Assessment Tools**.

- I'll describe the application of this process, for both the Coach and the Team, in the sections titled
    - **The Coach: Who is your Leader?**
    - **The Team: Who are your team members?**

- I'll provide an example case study to illustrate the process (specifically, as it relates to the Coach) in **Knowing the Coach**.

- I'll give a brief **Summary of the Knowing Process.**

- I'll recap the recommended insight mechanisms in the section titled **The Tools**.

- I'll provide Worksheets and Exercises you should use.

- Finally, at the end of this **Chapter Five**, I'll present the next two Implementation Checklists. These should be used as a basis for team discussion, as the next step toward implementing **(GT)** within your organization.
    - **Knowing the Coach,**
    - **Knowing the Team.**

The Interpersonal Insight Process

The Knowing the Coach case study (presented later in this chapter) represents the type of process to which we must all be open in order to create effective team and group functioning. That example illustrates the use of interpersonal insights in a specific team-based work environment. As depicted in the example, this Interpersonal Insight Process can be emotionally challenging. Still, the effort is extremely beneficial — for both the individual and the organization.

Before beginning this essential undertaking, be aware of the following considerations.

- **We all have our blind spots,** and need feedback to identify those blind spots and minimize their impact on ourselves and others. (Daniel Goleman provides an excellent discussion of the feedback necessity in the work environment in *Working with Emotional Intelligence.* He expands on this theme for leaders and top executives in *Primal Leadership.* These titles are both recommended to the reader in **References**, page 124.)

- **The example presented is not uniquely related to** this aspect of human functioning.

- **This is not easy.** As a clinical psychologist, I am well aware of this reality. Readers should also be aware that recognizing these challenging areas, receiving feedback about them, attempting to minimize their impact and to develop compensatory skills can be an emotionally painful process.

- **It is also a process in which we all must engage.** And the result has implications far beyond the world of work (although it has dramatic implications within this world).

- **Consider this alternative to the challenges of the personal learning process:** What if we were never given feedback about our challenging areas or never attempted to explore these areas? Wouldn't that constitute a much deeper experience of emotional pain and isolation?

- **The teambuilding process is not intended to become an "encounter group."** There must, however, be a process from which people in organizations and teams can receive constructive feedback in an appropriate and SUPPORTIVE manner, designed to help the individual and the greater organization.

- **There must be openness** to creating team structures that focus on constructive feedback among members, as well as training and coaching processes that support these goals.

- **Monitoring procedures** to track the effectiveness of and satisfaction with these supportive processes are required.

- **The temptation is to ignore these feedback aspects** because they can be uncomfortable. Not to give feedback, however, is an extremely damaging business mistake — directly affecting the bottom line.

- **Team members' abilities to interact harmoniously depend on a feedback loop** that promotes understanding and the acceptance of differences. This harmonious functioning <u>is</u> the business bottom line, because it will likely mean the difference between peak performance and mediocrity. (Once again, the reader is directed to Dr. Goleman's writings on the place of feedback in promoting peak performance in *Working with Emotional Intelligence* and in *Primal Leadership*.)

- **The absence of this harmonious function** makes this major part of our lives less tolerable and, at times, unbearable. Once again, these conditions have an obvious negative impact upon workplace goal attainment.

- **These and other increased workplace stressors directly impact** general health and attendance and may also notably affect employee retention. With so much at stake, support of these types of processes is well worth the investment.

As you can see, there are ample reasons to invest in the Interpersonal Insight Process. To achieve a maximized return, the process must be conducted professionally and the findings must be used wisely. The next sub-section provides basic direction to the reader about how to ensure this result.

Overview for the Use of Assessment Tools

I highly recommend utilizing a coaching / consulting professional for this *knowing* process. These professionals are a vital component in the effective execution of the **(GT)** model. Direct and structured discussions related to working styles and preferences should guide this process. Specifically, the use of workplace related inventories are designed to augment this learning experience.

- **These inventories will give a common framework** for discussion with the team. They will eventually assist the team members with their individual coaching process (formal or informal).

- **The consulting / coaching professional should have training** and expertise in the use of the Myers-Briggs Type Indicator® and other growth-oriented assessment tools (or have access to these services). (Myers-Briggs Type Indicator, MBTI, Myers-Briggs, and Introduction to Type are trademarks or registered trademarks of the Myers-Briggs Type Indicator Trust.)

- **This model puts forth the MBTI** as the basic building-block for knowing teams and their interactive qualities.

- **The MBTI is essential to this process.** A more thorough exploration, however, could also include accepted measures of emotional intelligence factors (both self-report and 360 degree instruments), and measures of specific leadership styles.

- **Appendix C** (page 115) will provide the reader with insight about these products and the professional services that should accompany them.

- **Appendix A** (page 109) specifically provides a detailed overview of the Myers-Briggs Type Indicator.

The reader can also visit the Consulting Psychologists Press website (www.cpp.com) for more specific information on the inventories discussed in this section and for general information on this type of assessment process (including links to qualified service providers of the MBTI).

It is important to note that these tools are inventories — not tests.

- **There are no right or wrong answers;** they merely explore preferences and interests.

- **Inventory data should never be utilized in a restricting or punitive manner.** It is unethical and illegal to make restrictive decisions based upon these results.

- **These tools are designed for a process of growth** and career / workplace enhancement. They must be utilized in this manner.

- **The results and feedback resulting from these tools** *must be given by trained professionals* with the utmost respect shown to each individual's sensitivities and desire for confidentiality.

- **The greatest potential for misuse** concerns the training and professional status of those who implement these services.

- **The use of appropriately trained professionals** to provide these types of assessment services gives greater assurances that they are used appropriately, both in the individual case, as well as within the larger organization. This is an undertaking that must be done with an experienced guide.

- **The original and detailed test results** are the property of the individual team member — and *are not for personnel or supervisory records.*

- **The utmost respect must be given** to each person's individuality and confidentiality in this process.

- **Notable protective guidelines are essential** basic premises for effective use of these tools. These guidelines must be implemented on a daily basis, as well as in any specialized training and / or coaching processes that the team members receive.

The American Psychological Association website (www.APA.org) can provide more information regarding the ethical use of these tools, as found in its Ethical Principles. My own organization, J. F. Zagotta & Associates, LLC, also provides more detailed information (including links) on usage and ethical issues related to these instruments and to the professional coaching / consulting process on our website (www.jfzassoc.com).

With these precautions and standards in place, the MBTI and other instruments are invaluable and highly rewarding / enriching tools to bring to the teambuilding process. Appendices A (page 109) and C (page 115) provide detailed descriptions of the tools available for use in these applications.

The Coach: Who Is Your Leader?

Before you get the idea that this process is easy to accomplish, let me, as a professional and licensed "*healer,*" dissuade you from that misapprehension.

- It takes a great deal of effort and is not without pain, on both personal and interpersonal levels.

- Establishing and maintaining highly efficient teams, like all human relationships, requires work! Although they are ultimately rewarding and worth the effort, don't fool yourself that this process is easy.

- *My gosh*, this sounds a lot like a marriage! The parallels may be frightening, but true.

- It is essential to gain a considerable level of self-knowledge and knowledge about those with whom you work.

- The coach must be the starting point because his or her behavior has the most impact and usually sets the overall tone for the team.

The process of *knowing* will start with considerations as it applies to the coach (as used in the context of a sports team, or the leader, supervisor, project manager — *the person with the ultimate authority and responsibility*). The discussion will then continue with a focus on how to apply this process with the team in both individual as well as group formats, and a recap of recommended tools to use.

I'll begin this discussion with the third example case study, continuing with the behavioral healthcare team used in the previous chapters. To reiterate, although the specific work setting may be different, the types of mistakes made by the coach and one possible path towards gaining insights and adjusting actions in light of these insights should seem quite familiar.

Knowing the Coach

For our discussion of *Knowing the Coach,* let me continue with the behavioral healthcare example I have been using and introduce this coach's experience of learning to know myself. As a coach, I brought strengths and weaknesses to the task of leading a team. I wish I had been more aware of these before I started the endeavor — particularly, the weaknesses. Later on in this chapter, recommended tools to use in this process of gaining self-knowledge are presented. The most important of these is the Myers Briggs Type Indicator (MBTI). Appendix A (page 109) provides background information on the MBTI for those who are unfamiliar with the instrument. I will use my MBTI profile as an example to illustrate the process of *Knowing the Coach.*

My personal MBTI profile is (I-Introversion), (N-Intuitive), (T-Thinking), (P-Perceptive) *INTP.* (See the Worksheets and Exercises later in this chapter for an overview of this MBTI *Type,* as well as the common associations and preferences corresponding to differing types.) My strengths as a professional can be summarized as follows.

- I am a skilled creator of structures and systems.

- I have strong abilities for making conduits and connections in physical and human systems, and have a knack for devising systemic solutions.

- I am fairly proficient at visualizing how a system will work and taking this visualization from idea, to paper, to implementation in a seamless manner.

- I generally do not allow emotional reactions or my own subjectivity to interfere with the task at hand and can effectively tune out issues during implementation that would cause the team to deviate from an objective plan.

- I can see possibilities in most situations, and usually land on my feet in navigating a system.

Ultimately, I believe I possess strengths in navigating human systems ranging from couples, to families, to teams, to larger organizations, and in developing unique systemic solutions. What I have just described, as those of you familiar with the MBTI may recognize, is a classic description of some of the strengths commonly associated with the *INTP Type.* Some people have very balanced profiles and draw on preferences across MBTI continuum dimensions. In contrast, my profile is a fairly pronounced *INTP.*

Within this context of discussing my strengths, I must also say that at the time I created this team, I was not particularly in touch with my weaknesses. As defined as some of my strengths were, my areas of challenge were equally as pronounced. With great effort, support and assistance, I believe I have improved on and compensated for these areas. The first step was recognizing my weaker — or in MBTI terms — my non-dominant preference areas. The literal name for my profile type — utilizing MBTI terms — would read: Introverted, Intuitive, Thinking, and

Perceptive. Some functioning challenges that can go along with this type (again, I'm a fairly pronounced example) are:

- I draw energy by being alone, being away from the team;

- I am not adept at breaking down the details (in my case, I am often *very* challenged by the details);

- I am often not tuned into the emotional aspects of group decision-making;

- I am frequently *flitting* around in search of new possibilities.

Keep in mind that I am highlighting *my* weaker functioning areas and some common pitfalls as they might be interpreted by the MBTI. These factors are not necessarily the same for all individuals of this MBTI *Type*.

So, during this period of less insight into my own impact on people, how did I help my team? I, at my best, helped the team navigate through the systems of our client families and our agency's bureaucracies with great ease. I helped prevent the team from getting bogged down in the trivialities and distractions of both systems. I helped maintain *Flow* via the very effective team process that we created. For the most part, this worked very well. Again, we caught on *fire* as a workgroup. Our small team was nearly more productive than the rest of our large department. We took on the most challenging cases, retained all our staff, and "LOVED" our work. We couldn't wait to come in, and we didn't want to go home (I don't suggest this as a goal for teambuilding — but it happened for our team).

We certainly faced some internal problems, however. Although each of us brought her or his own challenges to the team, my challenges as the coach had a more profound impact on the team and set the overall tone for the group.

When things did not go so well, I would ride rough shod over members' emotional reactions. I did realize they actually had emotional reactions, but I could not imagine what they were reacting to or how a work process would even evoke emotional reactions. I would have great ideas but not be able to articulate their rationale, and I usually did not realize the importance of doing so. I would say things like, "Oh, you'll see," or "just trust me." You can imagine how well that worked. I would often be quite scattered by possibilities, at the expense of the task at hand.

While our overall experience was generally very rewarding and productive, these are the things we usually struggled with. Again, as the coach, I set the tone. Hence, the key issues were usually mine or those of people reacting to me. I hasten to add that with this team's help and my personal developmental efforts, I *have* improved on and compensated for these areas. Our team started out well, was able to overcome my weaknesses as a coach, and went on to function as a great example of Guerilla Teambuilding **(GT)**.

I would summarize this particular behavioral health team example as follows.

First, this is a fairly typical illustration of how interaction styles impact a team process. This is particularly true of the coach's interaction style. It is further a good opportunity to give the reader a tangible example of how to operationalize the MBTI constructs.

Secondly, this is also a good example of the power of the team process and its ability to circumvent some of the day-to-day interaction challenges we all face. And, it illustrates the areas where this process can go wrong.

Third, the reader should see from this example that an area of challenge usually indicates the existence of a corresponding "end of the continuum" that represents a particular strength. *Every coin has two sides!*

Finally, the MBTI is presented as a tool that proves very useful in understanding your preferred ways of doing things, in understanding differences in people, in avoiding villainization of others and, instead, in accepting – even celebrating — these differences.

Personally, I have found the MBTI to be a validation of strengths and individuality. I will emphasize, again, that it is a fantastic teambuilding tool. I believe my *"Journey"* (if you will) towards these understandings is fairly typical of what can be expected by implementing the process I describe. After many years, along with additional insights and personal successes, I find the lessons of this period, and my own personal blind spots quite amusing — as do most of my colleagues who participated in this initial teambuilding experience. You live — you learn (hopefully)!

A coach **must** undergo a personal exploration related to knowing herself or himself. I specifically recommend that the coach obtain the services of a coaching / consulting professional in undertaking this process. Although an in-depth discussion of this *coaching the coach* process would at least require the addition of another chapter (if not a separate book), I do present a brief overview of the general coaching process for those readers unfamiliar with these professional services in Appendix B, page 113.

What I have discovered concerning the importance of this learning process, first and foremost for the *coach,* can be summarized as follows:
1. As I gradually compensate for my weaknesses, one of which has been a lack of awareness related to the feelings of others, I have found that a little more consensus building, and a little more one-to-one check-ins have gone a long way in avoiding major "fires" down the road (fires that I, *the coach,* had caused).
2. As I spend less time putting out "fires", and less time fixing my own mistakes, I am able to spend more time on the tasks that only I can provide for the teams I manage. As team members focus and specialize on the tasks that they excel at, it is my job to maintain their *Flow* by doing what only I

can do, moving obstacles that get in their way. Naturally occurring obstacles prove tough enough without adding to them with ones you create.

3. If the *coach* is not performing the tasks that I just mentioned, then they are not getting the job done. Only the leader can be monitoring the entire operation and ensuring the team has what it needs. This is inherent by definition. If team members are left to monitor these overview tasks, then they will not spend time in their "superstar" or assistive roles that the team process requires (and that you created). Your work becomes pointless. Hence, the *coach's* process of gaining personal insights, of building strengths, and of leveraging and compensating for weaknesses is the most important. Others can be found within the team to play the various roles, even the superstar roles, but no one can substitute for the *coach*. The only options for failure at this level is to get rid of the old *coach*, and bring in a new one.

4. The process reminds me of watching Bozo's Circus as a child. Every so often, and probably too often, the actual circus act on Bozo was the guy who could keep about 7 or 8 plates spinning on sticks. All his efforts were focused on keeping each one spinning, recognizing which ones were slowing down and about to fall, and giving them just the spin or extra boost needed to keep them going. If this *plate guy* were focused on some other minutiae, or his own personal issues, or off creating problems in some other arena, he or she could not keep their focus on the one singular, and vitally important task they had (which no one else could do for them — because only they were the *plate guy*), to keep those plates spinning! It was a selfless job. Only the *plate guy* stood between the spinning plates and the unforgiving forces of gravity. Only he could ensure that the unnatural process of plates spinning in the air was maintained, and all the hopes of those plates accomplishing their goals, and the entire final product of entertaining the audience by perpetuating this gravity defying feat rested with him. The *plate guy* had to know her or his own issues, put them aside, and perform the task that only she or he could. "I am not a plate, I am a *plate guy*, and those plates are counting on me". I should hope this individual was the first to go through the personal insight process (and learn from it) — if I were a *plate*!

Knowing The Team

- **A coach** may be called upon to manage and enhance the functioning of an existing team, or to select and manage a new team (to complete ongoing functions or to accomplish a short-term goal).

- **Knowing these members,** and *team members knowing each other,* will be critical to the effective functioning of the team. There are many ways to accomplish these goals.

The following model, designed to structure the task of *Knowing the Team,* provides some tools to catalyze — and, yes, speed up — the process.

1. **One-to-One**

- **Knowing each team member** on an individual basis is an important task.

- **There is no substitute** for one-to-one time in accomplishing this goal.

- **One-to-one coaching formula.** This time allows the coach and the team member to:
    - learn the *preferences, strengths,* and *aspirations* of the other;
    - *discover the most effective ways to communicate*;
    - *accomplish shared goals*;
    - and *delineate, clarify, and coordinate team and individual goals.*

- **Introducing the coach.** It is useful for the coach to explain their standard methods as a coach upfront.
    - To outline the coach's strengths.
    - To describe what the coach can add to the team.
    - To describe how the coach can help members to accomplish both the teams and their own individual aspirations.

- **No finger shaking.** This presentation should not be made in a dogmatic manner, describing "This is who I am, and you better deal with it."

- **This introduction process accomplishes the following.**
    - Educates team members about the coach.
    - Promotes confidence in the coach's abilities.
    - Asks team members for help with the coach's challenging areas.
    - Models the openness and personal insights that will be crucial to team success.

- **This is a process, not an event.** The coach should inquire the same of each team member and be an intent listener to members' views of these issues on an ongoing basis.

- **Spend Time on this process.** How these issues impact on day-to-day and longer term functioning is an important aspect of team meetings.

- **Spelling it out.** A format for this interaction entitled Worksheet 1, *Coach & Team Member Discussion Format* appears later in this chapter (page 61).

2. **Assessment**

- **What's good for the goose...** The assessment process outlined for the coach is also appropriate for the team.

- **The MBTI is recommended for use with the entire team.** This Team MBTI is best done in both an individual and group format. Team members can share this insightful experience and can immediately begin to utilize the information to promote stronger team functioning.

- **The MBTI is the most common teambuilding tool** used for organizational enhancement. It is utilized by hundreds of corporations, companies, and not-for-profit organizations on a regular basis.

- **This MBTI experience will provide a common framework** for the entire team to discuss members' differences and styles. It will also help define work tasks and assignments based upon individual strengths and preferences.

- **This MBTI experience will also facilitate leveraging strengths** among team members. It is crucial for creating and maintaining *Flow* (more to come on this topic in **Chapter Six**, page 77).

- **The MBTI is a nearly indispensable means of implementing** this process. It makes the process of "fitting together" much easier. Several other tools mentioned in Appendix C (page 115) may play a useful role in accomplishing the same end, whether used early on or later in the teambuilding process. The MBTI, however, is the recommended starting point. The other measures mentioned in Appendix C blend nicely with the MBTI, and a more useful picture emerges after using them together.

- **The combination of the MBTI and these other measures** form the building-blocks of an ongoing, interactive knowledge program. They thus create their own Visual Operations Plan for navigating such an endeavor.

The MBTI as a group activity deserves some additional focus and elaboration. Many people have participated in one or possibly several MBTI presentations in their workplace. All too often participants remember almost nothing about their personal profile, because it was not integrated into their work, or their team, or in helping to choose a good assignment fit for them. The results often are only utilized as an interesting aside. The goal of these presentations should be for each participant to take away a sense of how their profile relates to that of the others who participated. In effect, each of these experiences can and should be a teambuilding exercise. But far too often, once the presentation or the team dissolves, the validity of that activity dissipates, and the participants do not continue to incorporate those findings into their personal development. This is a mistake, and one that the **(GT)** program attempts to extinguish. The Group MBTI process is a teambuilding exercise, and a springboard into the **(GT)** meeting structure, and 80/20 role-based assignments.

You don't just end with knowing your profiles. You use this information to make plans, as well as to structure your team in optimally efficient, productive, and supportive ways. With reference, again, to the 80/20 process, the MBTI plays a big role by ensuring that there is a common language for knowing each team member. The *Coach's* participation is hence vital, because the *coach* is a member of the team, Thus, the *coach* can bring tremendous strengths and resources to the process — as a team member who has gone through these steps, has improved his functioning as a result, and who can model engaging oneself into the process. The team must integrate all its members into this learning process, including the leader. And, besides being a valuable learning opportunity, a group MBTI presentation is *fun*, and a great bonding experience. One that all team members should take part in.

Summarizing the Knowing Process

This *Knowing the Team* model — One-to-One Coach & Team Member Discussion plus Team MBTI Assessment — complements the *Knowing the Coach* process. Together, these *Knowing* activities provide a vital "inventory" of strengths and skills that the entire team will learn to leverage for mutual advantage. *Knowing* provides the whole team with fundamental insights for understanding team roles.

This knowledge comprises the catalog of component building-blocks for strengths and skill sets of the team. This understanding can be used by team members in the same way that the Visual Operations Plan is used by the service provider serving as a navigation hub. In this case, each team member knows which team members possess the strengths and skills to assist in any given task. The Coach must be especially well-versed in this understanding, because the Coach makes the initial task assignments. Good initial assignments will minimize the need for team members to seek additional resources when completing assignments.

The key lies in *Knowing*.

The Tools

To accomplish the goals of knowing the team and the coach, a number of useful aids and illustrations appear on the remaining pages of **Chapter Five**. These tools are described as follows:

- **Tools for coaches to use** in gaining an overview of the various MBTI factors, their corresponding *fit* with various work task assignments, and ways to work with and coach individuals operating out of these various factors are provided in the Worksheets.
  - o **Coach & Team Member Discussion Format**, Worksheet 1, on page 61.
  - o **Coaching**, Worksheet 2, page 63.
  - o **Goal Completion Task Assignments by MBTI Preference Strengths**, Worksheet 3, page 65.
- **Exercises 1 through 4** (pp. 67 — 70) provide structures that will help implement group planning and facilitate problem solving discussions which involve task assignments related to MBTI types and preferences for individual team members.
  - o **Exercise 1** (page 67) provides a review of each MBTI type and associated functions. This will help to orient team members to the task assignment activity.

o **Exercise 2** (page 68) offers a general overview of the type factors and corresponding preferences. This should be used to commence a loosely structured discussion and planning session on the topic.

o **Exercise 3** (page 69) provides a more structured format that should lead a team through identification of strengths and preferences of members, and the formal assignment of complementary work roles.

o **Exercise 4** (page 70) represents a specific application example of Exercise 3. Here a coach has determined the functions and attributes needed to accomplish an assigned project. These work roles are then coordinated to best fit within a team of individuals who represent an existing workgroup (rather than selecting a totally new workgroup uniquely for this particular project).

- **The MBTI Factors, Figures 8, 9, and 10**, pages 71 — 73, are designed to be used as discussion aids during this process. They provide a visual model for describing the process of fitting together team members' various preferences and strengths.

- **Implementation Checklists 3 and 4** are provided on pages 74 and 75. These should be used as a basis for team discussion, as the next steps toward implementing **(GT)** within your organization.

Worksheet 1

Coach & Team Member Discussion Format

Coach

Who am I?_____

_____

_____

What are my strengths?_____

_____

_____

What are my greatest challenges and areas for growth?_____

_____

_____

Team Member

Who am I?_____

_____

_____

What are my strengths?_____

_____

_____

What are my greatest challenges and areas for growth? _____

_____

_____

Interaction Plan

What must we be aware of regarding each other in order to promote an optimal working relationship?

Coach _____

_____

_____

Team Member_____

_____

_____

Worksheet 1
Coach & Team Member Discussion Format

Additional Notes:

Worksheet 2

Coaching

Introverted

- Make sure you offer plenty of one-to-one time.
- Allow them structured time away from the team to achieve goals.
- Do check-ins during team meetings: they may hesitate to share good ideas or important feedback.
- Draw them out in a respectful and comfortable way.
- Remember, their strength will relate to tasks that require introspection, self-knowledge, and internal analysis. Often, these tasks are overlooked: structure assignments to ensure utilization of this valuable resource.

Extroverted

- Ensure they have a group forum.
- Minimize solitary work assignments.
- Ensure they do not dominate team discussions: appropriately channel their team-based role.
- Pair with a high "I" team member to accentuate each member's strengths.
- Remember, their strength will be as the spokesperson or the marketer for the group to the outside: structure tasks to utilize this strength.

Sensing

- Keep assignments based upon data and information retrieval.
- Don't overwhelm with "big picture" tasks.
- Allow ample avenues and resources with which to retrieve information.
- Remember, their strength lies in being the sensory input from the outer world to the group: give them the tools with which to perform this task.

Intuitive

- Keep assignments focused on the structural overview and the big picture.
- Do not overwhelm with assignments concerned with fact retrieval.
- Integration, analysis, and synthesis are notable preferences and strengths; utilize accordingly.
- Pairing an intuitive with an "S" (one who creates data for analysis) can accentuate the strengths of both.

Worksheet 2
Coaching

Thinking

- Keep assignments logical and sequential.

- Minimize feeling and subjective value basis of their assignments and tasks.

- Objectivity, logic, compliance with rules and standards, and fairness are their strengths: assign tasks accordingly.

- Useful in keeping the team on track and following a logical sequence: structure their role to maximize this strength for the team.

- Pairing with a "Feeling" may provide the strength of balancing logical task accomplishment procedures with group harmony and morale.

Feeling

- Maintaining harmony and cohesion within the group is a strength.

- Set goals and assignments that are in tune with their values.

- Discuss values and feelings towards task assignments in order to relate a sense of "fit" and purpose.

- A positive "ethical divining rod."

Judging

- Decisiveness is a strength: structure role to maximize this strength for the team in maintaining focus.

- Can assist with breaking down group ideas into sequential steps for implementation: structure roles and assignments accordingly.

- May be frustrated by delays, chaos, change, and unpredictability: structure roles to limit this, and counsel patience.

- Pairing them with a strong "P" may maximize the strengths of each party. Combination of flexibility, possibility, and focus.

Perceiving

- Strength in creative solutions and adaptation.

- Likely the best team members in dealing with and managing change: Structure their roles, tasks, and assignments accordingly.

- Don't stifle with highly structured agendas or methods of accomplishing tasks / assignments.

- Can be very effectively utilized by taking a lead in problem-solving discussions.

Worksheet 3

Goal Completion Task Assignments by MBTI Preference Strengths

Introversion

- Willing to do the solitary time on tasks. _____

- Have the strength of contemplation. _____

- Need periodic solitude and separation from the group. _____

Extroversion

- Good spokesperson. _____

- Initiate discussions. _____

- Presenter of team ideas to the greater organization / public. _____

- Thrive on continual interaction. _____

Sensing

- Data collection; bringing facts, statistics, etc. to the group. _____

- Group librarians and archivists (keeping of records). _____

- Do not overwhelm with "big picture" or conceptual tasks. _____

Intuitive

- "Big picture" and conceptualization. _____

- Integrate data for the team. _____

- Analyze trends and forecasts. _____

- Form cognitive connections in system._____

- Do not overwhelm with data collection, facts, or specifics. _____

Worksheet 3

Goal Completion Task Assignments by MBTI Preference Strengths

Thinking
- Objectivity and fairness in decision-making. _____
- Implementation of logical processes. _____
- Not easily panicked. _____
- Don't overwhelm with issues of harmony or emotion. _____

Feeling
- Conscience and spirit for the team. _____
- Maintenance of team relationships. _____
- Support and motivational energy. _____
- Allow a crucial role in maintaining team harmony. _____
- Do not overwhelm with "the rules" and "the facts." _____

Judging
- Decisiveness and crisis management skills. _____
- Scheduler and task maintainer. _____
- Developing the steps for achieving goals. _____
- Do not overwhelm with possibilities. _____

Perceiving
- Seizing on opportunities. _____
- Flexible and adaptive. _____
- *Brainstormer* and source of novel solutions. _____
- Development and project start-up. _____
- Do not overwhelm with prescribed steps / traditional view _____

Teambuilding Exercise 1

MBTI Type Identification

Fill the Name and letter of the appropriate MBTI Factor in the blank.

Relationship Building	Values
Harmony	Cohesion
Morale	
Convictions	
_____	

Rules	Regulations
Standards	Policy
Objectivity	Procedure
Implementation	
_____	

Conceptual	Integration
Conduits	Connections
Analyze	Forecasts
Trends	
Patterns	
_____	

Develop	Horizons
Research	Opportunity
Change	Adaptation
Resourceful	
Creativity	
_____	

Spokesperson	Networker
Facilitator	Presenter
Verbal	Marketer
Social Context	
_____	

Self-Knowledge	Introspection
Awareness	Independent
Inner-World	
_____	

Data	Facts	Collection
Librarian	Data Entry	Editor
Proofreader	Sources	Researched
Archivist		
Observation		
_____		

Predictable	Orderly
Structured	Timely
Measured	Decisive
Scheduled	Reliable
Order	
_____	

Teambuilding Exercise 2

Task Roles

Each MBTI factor has roles that create an expected fit for the preferences of those displaying various MBTI profiles. This graphic can be used as a guide for discussing and recording task assignments of teams and individual members.

Introversion	Extroversion	Sensing	Intuitive
Completion of solitary tasks	Public Spokes-person.	Data Collection and gathering	Integration of information
Assignments calling for introspection and contemplation	Discussion facilitator	Data Entry	Conceptualization
	Networker	Librarian and archivist	Systems creation and assessment
Assignments requiring self-knowledge	Marketer	Fact finder and checker	Forecaster and trend analyzer
		Proofreader	Conduits and connection points
Thinking	**Feeling**	**Judging**	**Perceiving**
Rules and policy interpreter	Harmony and cohesion in relationships	Decisiveness	Opportunity procurement
Objective decision-making		Commitment	Innovations and possibilities
	Support and enthusiasm	Day-by-Day planning	
Fairness and impartiality	Human connections	Structure and organizations	Development of new ideas
Logical processes			Creative /Flexible
	Conscience and value based decisions	Creation of steps and procedures	Change management

Teambuilding Exercise 3

Team Assignments

Instructions

1. List the validated types for each team member.
2. Below this type, identify the prominent task functions this team member prefers from the boxes (or record applicable functions not listed).
3. Make team function assignments, and record them below member's name.

Introspection Self-Knowledge Awareness Independent Inner-World	Spokesperson Networker Facilitator Presenter Verbal Marketer Social-Context	Rules Regulations Standards Policy Objectivity Procedure Implementation	Relationship- Building Values Harmony Cohesion Morale Convictions
I	**E**	**T**	**F**

Decisive Orderly Structured Measured Predictable Reliable Scheduled Timely	Data / Facts Collection Data Entry Librarian Archivist Editor Proofreader Sources Researched	Conceptual Integration Conduits Connections Analyze Forecasts Trends Patterns	Develop Horizons Research Opportunity Change Adaptation Resourceful Creativity
J	**S**	**N**	**P**

ISTJ (_____)   ISFJ (_____)   INFJ (_____)   INTJ (_____)
_____   _____   _____   _____
_____   _____   _____   _____

ISTP (_____)   ISFP (_____)   INFP (_____)   INTP (_____)
_____   _____   _____   _____
_____   _____   _____   _____

ESTP (_____)   ESFP (_____)   ENFP (_____)   ENTP (_____)
_____   _____   _____   _____
_____   _____   _____   _____

ESTJ (_____)   ESFJ (_____)   ENFJ (_____)   ENTJ (_____)
_____   _____   _____   _____
_____   _____   _____   _____

Teambuilding Exercise 4

Example Assignment Exercise

1. Area I displays the tasks and attributes that the Coach has determined will be needed. These were taken from the boxes in Teambuilding Exercise 2.

2. Area II represents the validated MBTI profiles of the team members charged with the tasks of this project. These were taken from the complete list of possible MBTI profiles in the lower half of Teambuilding Exercise 3.

3. Discuss with the team the best preferential fit for assignments within the project, and write the assigned role for each member under her or his name and validated MBTI Profile indication.

Area I	**Area II**
Values	ISTJ (_____)
Morale	_____
Opportunity	_____
Resourceful	_____
Analyze	
Conduits	EFSP (_____)
Policy	_____
Regulations	_____
Procedure	_____
Verbal	
Introspection	INFP (_____)
Independent	_____
Inner-World	_____
Data Entry	_____
Facts	
Sources	ENTP (_____)
Archivist	_____
Structured	_____
Scheduled	_____
	ENFJ (_____)
	_____
	_____
	_____

Figure 8

MBTI Factors

- The Team viewed as a singular entity comprised of MBTI factors. The various team members house the skills and functions, joining together to make a singular identity.

- This figure can serve as a visual means of displaying team role and task assignments, with different team members assigned to different functions of the team

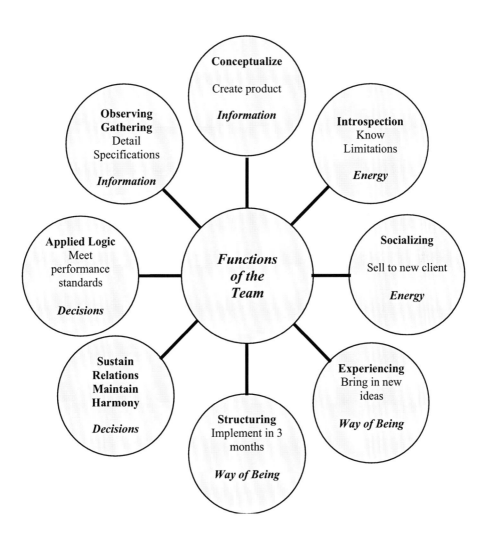

Figure 9

MBTI Factors — Individual

- Figure 9 depicts a single individual and her or his identified MBTI Type.

- Every individual possesses all of the functioning attributes across all MBTI Factors, but relies mostly upon particular areas of strength — the dominant factors.

- Imagine that performing tasks in your non-preferred or non-dominant factor areas is like performing physical tasks with your non-dominant hand.

Figure 10

MBTI Factors Exercise

- Figure 10 provides a visual example of all the functions of the MBTI. All functions are present for all individuals. However, as presented in Figure 9, each individual has a set pattern of preferences for the functions she or he utilizes most readily and easily.

- Figure 10 can be used as an exercise in which an individual can mark the functions that she or he prefers and utilizes more readily. This can serve as a loose guide for type evaluation and as a comparison tool to explore with actual MBTI results for profile validation purposes.

- Make a copy of this Figure for each team member. On each copy, highlight the individual's MBTI Type in yellow.

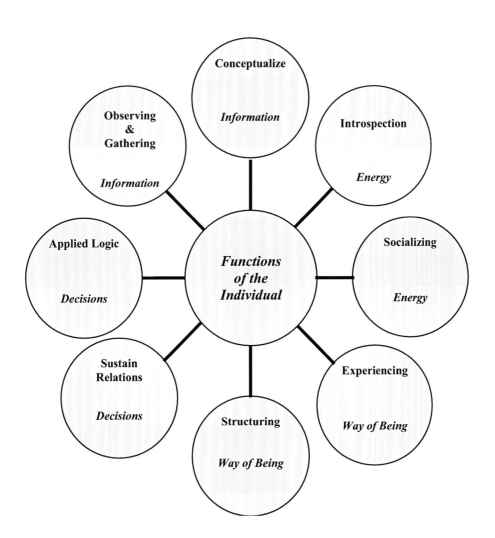

Implementation Checklist 3

Knowing the Coach

- Has the coach sought out a coaching professional to learn about her or his own styles and practices?

- Identify a qualified coaching professional who has specific skills in and / or access to services appropriately utilizing the Myers Briggs Type Indicator and other supportive preference and interest inventories, such as emotional intelligence measures, leadership style inventories, and 360-degree assessments.

- Institute assessment plans using resources found in the previous two bullets.

- Work with a coach to identify a learning plan based upon this information.

- Develop a presentation and / or list of your strengths and preferences as a coach and of your areas of non-dominant function or challenges.

- Create a presentation to utilize with team members in making them aware of your skills and attributes as well as your challenges within the coaching process.

Notes:

Implementation Checklist 4

Knowing the Team

- Conduct individualized meetings between the coach and each team member to acquaint each other with respective interpersonal styles, strengths, technical skills, and compatibility in the work environment and team process.

- The coach should model openness and the ability to comfortably and constructively discuss differences in these individualized meetings.

- Use a trained professional certified in using the Myers Briggs Type Indicator within a teambuilding context. Use such a professional in an ongoing teambuilding consultation role for the group.

- Utilize the information from the MBTI. Not in the form of printouts, but in the form of discussions regarding information the group members have learned related to themselves and each other. Review team members' preferences, strengths, and challenges to negotiate appropriate assignment areas based upon this information.

- Ensure that each team member is familiar with the preferences, strengths and non-dominant / challenge areas for the other members.

- As a team, develop plans and task assignments that maximize these strengths.

- Maximize team members' cultural diversities as strengths in the process indicated previously. Include regular time in meetings to review the effectiveness of the team interaction process.

- Utilize continuous performance improvement, not only related to mechanical actions and to documents / intellectual property production, but also applied to the interaction process in the team.

- Utilize technology to maximize effective communication and access among team members.

Notes:

Chapter Six

OHIO, *Flow* and OTF Management Models

OHIO

The term OHIO is an acronym for "Only Handle It Once." This model describes systems and practices which ensure that the user does just that (see Illustration 4, page 41). The value is obvious.

- **The applications are endless.** "OHIO" has been used by
  - those who coach adults with Attention Deficit Hyperactivity Disorder (ADHD) (see Hallowell, *Driven to Distraction*, 1994),
  - those who have applied it to methods for handling the "in-box,"
  - and those establishing procedures for computer data input.
- **A process can always be more "OHIO."** "OHIO" is a saying similar to "a stitch in time…"
- **Within Guerrilla Teams, OHIO functioning is crucial to create, preserve, and maintain *Flow*.** We'll describe *Flow* in more detail in the next sub-section. *Flow* describes a state of peak performance that athletes call "the Zone". And *Flow* has spiritual and meditative parallels as well.

The main presentation in this sub-section will focus on making decisions, although OHIO has a host of implications for the entire teambuilding process.

- **The OHIO model requires the team to make decisions *right-then-and-there,*** while key members are present. Hence, you're only handling the issues once! This eliminates equivocation and endless deliberation.
- **Eventually, you're going to try *something*** and see how it goes. But, making decisions "only once" can cause some anxiety: "Maybe we should think about this more?" "What if we're wrong? "
- **Efficiency over anxiety.** The anxieties caused by not revisiting decisions pale in comparison to the gains harvested by increased efficiency.
- **Ultimately, poor decisions made in this process are obviated.** If you make a poor decision under the OHIO model — it simply means that you will face a new decision later (not that you are revisiting an old one).
- **Decisive mistakes are okay.** You will undoubtedly make some mistakes – no matter what process you use – and you will sometimes act more quickly than you might prefer. That's okay.
- **Think of OHIO as extolling an experimental method.** You collect data and make a decision. You monitor the outcomes, collect more data, and then either decide to stay with your current plans or to revise them.
- **OHIO is an ongoing process** — "Continuous Performance Improvement" and / or Kaizen exemplified.

Illustration 6

OHIO

O nly

No Waste

H andle

No
Indecision

I t

No Delays

O nce

No
Repeating

Consider these additional implications of the suggested decisiveness.

- **Decisions for Better or Worse.** If, in the presence of its members, the team decides to take a certain action, then the team lives with that decision.

- **Learn From Successes and Mistakes.** The team may need to re-analyze a situation, including any negative consequences that occur from a decision, and to make a new decision.

- **Ultimate Efficiency.** This process, however, is still more efficient than lengthy deliberation, decision-making bit by bit, or setting a date to meet about making a decision, and later, finalizing the steps toward that decision. This last process (the "Anti-OHIO" Model) negatively affects and possibly destroys *Flow*.

- **Peak Performance Rules!** One of the major premises of Guerrilla Team-building **(GT)** is that *Flow* is crucial. People working at their peak massively outperform others–even themselves–when they are not in *Flow*.

- **Maintaining *Flow*.** As the coach, your first and foremost job is to maintain *Flow*. You will not find a more motivational tool, nor one that provides greater performance-enhancement.

- **Added Steps Diminish *Flow*.** If you put five steps into a process that could be done with one step, that's bad "OHIO" practice. It impedes *Flow*.

- **More Steps, More Effort.** If you put five steps into a process that members could do with one, that makes it more likely the task will not get accomplished. At minimum, it will require further monitoring and control efforts to ensure it does get done.

- **A Universal Truth.** Remember Murphy's Law: "anything that can go wrong, will". Every superfluous step added to a process gives Murphy one more chance.

- **Keep it Simple.** The mistakes you will make by only handling things once are far less important than the impediments and inefficiency of hesitant handling in a process, decision, or action — not to mention the ever-increasing probability that things "will go wrong".

Be aware that decisiveness is only a first step. The emphasis on decisions is intended to help you get off to a quick start, but it's only one application of OHIO. Make sure that you don't stop there. Take action!

I've already urged you to make meetings more productive by creating physical deliverables before you disperse. Keep up the good work. Decide what the team is going to do, then do it! Remember the "experimental method". It is, quite literally, better to do the wrong thing than to do nothing. Even if you are wrong, you've gained knowledge and experience. You can't lose – *Do Something!*

Illustration 7

OHIO – Violation

The OHIO Violation is represented by the following:

- Constant movement of projects or tasks to and from departments.

- Delayed feedback between groups compromising completion and implementation.

- Various points at which departments may repeat the same efforts.

- Lack of proximity between workgroups requiring extra steps to revise and /or make corrections.

First to the Thinkers

Then to the Movers & Shakers

Then to the Runners

Back to the Thinkers

Over to the Designers

Back to the Thinkers

Illustration 8

OHIO – Implementation

The OHIO Implementation is represented by the following:

- All involved parties present in one proximity.

- Feedback and corrections can be immediately incorporated.

- Meeting time involves development, creation, and implementation of the project.

- Duplication of efforts and time delays caused by department-to-department transferring of information and revisions are eliminated.

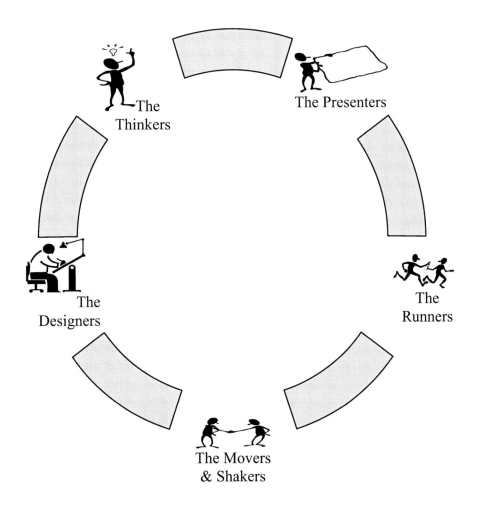

All tasks can be handled on a Right-Then-and-There basis.

The importance of technology to the OHIO and *Flow* models

The last quarter of the 20th century provided an explosion of enabling technologies. Telephony, media, computer applications and personal productivity technologies abound. Yet very few people or organizations do more than "scratch the surface" of these capabilities. And we don't just ignore the esoteric features of these technologies. In the vast majority of situations, we don't even try to use technology to leverage our human abilities.

For Guerrilla Teams, this has to change. Guerrilla Teambuilding **(GT)** is about enabling human resources. That's what technology does. Start by considering these thoughts.

- **Tools with a Purpose.** Think of technology as tools that maximize OHIO and produce *Flow*.

- **It's the User, Not the Tool.** If used appropriately, and in an integrated fashion, technology eliminates steps for providing needed information, gives key people instant access, and allows for timely feedback and / or monitoring related to effectiveness.

- **Tools Should Solve Problems, Not Create Them.** When technology works poorly, it adds steps and slows things down. A technology person should be part of your team – not an aside or somewhere to go to get something.

- **A Common Mistake:** The most common mistake is that the idea / applications people and the technology people occupy two separate worlds. They are not integrated. This situation can wreak havoc with *Flow*.

That said, please proceed only under the following restriction: *Do not deploy new technologies until your team has wrung every last productivity gain out of the technology you already own.* Unless the Guerrilla Team's goal is actually to deploy a new technology, such a deployment would probably be a distraction. Pursue only the goals defined for the team, but use technology to accelerate that pursuit.

This is where an information technology team member can often be useful. Their role should be to guide the use of existing technologies to improve team functions. Their purpose is to know, and share, *what's possible*. Remember, you must use what you already own before acquiring new "toys". However, you probably own (or have access to) more technologies than you imagine. Ask your information technology team member what your capabilities are in the following areas (and then ask what else is available).

- **Teleconferencing and Video Conferencing.** Teams should meet face-to-face, but what about temporary experts? If you have a phone and / or computer, you probably have access to these technologies.

- **Voice and Video Recording – Part I.** How much of what you need to know is already recorded? Team consumption of such material is far more productive than individual review. Your organization may have audio-visual equipment. If not, the telephone and computer can also be used. Have you considered all possible sources of *free* information: your own organization's archives, vendors, consultants, the internet, the local library?

- **Voice and Video Recording – Part II.** How much of what you need to capture might best be recorded this way? Remember that many people are auditory or visual learners. If you have a message to send, consider these media. Again, existing audio-visual equipment and computer technology may already exist.

- **Computer applications.** Chances are good that your organization uses at least some computer applications that are less than 10 years old. If so, your information technology team member can advise you about surprising ways that you can use existing application capabilities. Modern applications are capable of multiple, tailored usages. And your usage can almost certainly be integrated with broader system capabilities. In fact, your needs may already be satisfied and you just need to get access to these features.

- **Personal Productivity.** Most personal productivity devices and applications include amazing team-enabling capabilities. Consider at least the following.
  - **E-mail.** Almost all e-mail applications include team sharing capabilities. Internet e-mail clients, organization e-mail software, and even text-messaging devices (e.g., personal digital assistants, wireless telephones, pagers) can do more than you probably know.
  - **Productivity Suites I.** Word processing, spreadsheet, database and presentation software packages include a vast array of features for recording and organizing captured information. In fact, many contain important information capture capabilities that are seldom utilized (e.g., optical character, handwriting and voice recognition features).
  - **Productivity Suites II.** Your organization may already own under-utilized licenses for "professional" productivity tools. Your information technology team member can advise you regarding the availability and uses of important project management, drawing, diagramming, publishing and financial management tools you may already own.
  - **Networks.** Networks are not just for IT. If your organization uses any local area network, chances are good that applications and capacity are available for you to greatly enhance team sharing capabilities.

And remember, your goal is to have the team use these technologies. Don't "hand off" your usage to the IT department. Integrate these capabilities in your Guerrilla Team. In summary, OHIO means making decisions in team meetings *right-then-and-there* and minimizing steps in a process. Think about how various technologies can leverage this process. To fully integrate the Guerrilla Teambuilding **(GT)** model, we should now discuss *Flow* in more detail.

Flow

Flow is a term popularized by author and psychologist Mihaly Csikszentmihalyi in his book of the same name (Simon & Schuster, 1991).

- **Defined.** *Flow* is a term used to describe a state of peak performance. More specifically, Csikszentmihalyi describes this phenomenon as a total absorption in activities performed in pursuit of a goal.

- **Broad Application.** Although his book focused on *Flow* as a foundation for optimal experience in the totality of life, the concepts presented bear similar implications for the portions of our lives spent in workplace pursuits.

- **Blurring of Distinctions.** Per Csikszentmihalyi, at peak *Flow,* individuals blur all distinctions between work and so-called recreational activity.

- **Age-Old Solutions.** In the book *Flow*, Csikszentmihalyi explains that these concepts are by no means new. They have their origins in religious and spiritual thought dating back to the beginnings of human civilization.

- **In a Nutshell.** Csikszentmihalyi merges the collective wisdom of past philosophers and theologians on this topic with modern scientific data that support these traditions. In doing so, Csikszentmihalyi presents key elements of the concept, including eight core principles that create *Flow* states related to human activity. A summary of these key points follows:

    A. 1/3 of our life is work, 1/3 of our life is free or leisure time, 1/3 of our life is maintenance activities (e.g., laundry).

    B. Usually this last third is wasted and viewed as drudgery. But those individuals who can create moment-to-moment goals for these necessary tasks can salvage enjoyment from these mundane activities.

    C. Csikszentmihalyi concedes that these practices will make laundry (my example, not necessarily his) more bearable and less like drudgery, but these practices will not necessarily guarantee an optimal experience.

The 8 major components that create *Flow*

These research-based components can be used to avoid trial and error attempts at producing *Flow* states, according to Csikszentmihalyi. General principles for making *Flow* moments possible are surprisingly uniform across cultures, professions, genders, and financial backgrounds. Csikszentmihalyi conducted over 8,000 interviews across diverse groups to identify these principles.

- **Know the tasks involved in an activity very clearly.** The goals of the activity must be clear, non-conflicting and not confusing. Like the rules in a game of chess or the steps involved with playing a musical instrument, this clarity of task promotes *Flow*, even if thousands of small steps are involved. *Flow* breaks down in everyday life most often because the steps are not clear.

- **Know every moment if one's actions are getting oneself closer to – or further from – the goal.** Immediate feedback! This feedback comes naturally when enjoying a game of tennis or when playing a musical instrument. Feedback provides moment-to-moment correction toward achieving the goal. Often, life is not structured to allow for this feedback. To the extent that we can provide frequent updates on performance, we optimize the state of *Flow*.

- **The challenges of the activity must match the skills of the person.** The enjoyment of an activity is based on your skill level. It is more enjoyable to play a game with someone of a similar ability level. Activities that are too advanced or too easy cause distractions. Being optimally proficient draws you into an activity. Meeting a task at an optimal ability level, and adjusting the task over time to meet one's changing ability level, promotes *Flow*.

- **Feeling focused and concentrated on what you are doing.** Duality of attention (or splitting of attention — thinking one thing but actually doing something else) is not present in *Flow*. *Flow* involves a focused beam of attention. When attention is concentrated, much more is accomplished. This singularity of focus is experienced as rewarding in and of itself.

- **As one effortlessly focuses, one is not distracted by everyday frustrations.** They are removed from attention. One cannot laugh and cry simultaneously (well, it's highly unlikely). One cannot worry and be in *Flow*. *Flow* is rewarding in and of itself. Full concentration in the present defines *Flow*, and hence other issues cannot compete for one's attention. In this sense, the *Flow* state is a powerful escape from day-to-day worries and drudgery. Work done in the *Flow* state can become an escape. An example of "escaping backwards" might involve using drugs or generally denying reality. *Flow* would represent an example of "escaping forward," that is, engaging in a positive activity that allows you to transcend.

- **Feeling that one can be in control of one's life.** In *Flow,* you are never in complete control but are somewhat on an edge or teetering on a fence. If you don't use your skills, you will fall off (i.e., not be successful). However, in *Flow* we feel we possess the skills needed to be successful. In *Flow*, while challenged, you know that you have the competence to do the task.

- **Loss of self-consciousness.** When people have to concentrate and use all their skills, self-consciousness is lost. Often, we are bothered when wondering what others think of us, worrying about others, or feeling self-consumed. In *Flow*, one does not have the luxury of these distractions. One loses the sense of self, being so consumed by the task at hand that self-consciousness disappears. In *Flow*, we feel we've gone beyond the self.

The experience is much like being in a choir or being on a team that is working well together. In these situations, you are no longer just a person but part of something greater. This going beyond yourself is an exhilarating experience! Once people leave the *Flow* experience, what they were able to accomplish actually promotes a stronger sense of self. An enhanced view of one's own skills and abilities can emerge that more strongly defines the individual.

- **A sense of time is transformed.** Often, we chop up our experience of time into small intervals. In *Flow,* our sense of time is compressed. The day goes by quickly. Hours seem like minutes, and minutes like seconds. In *Flow,* rathe   )ped up time intervals, one finds time adapted to   sense of time is changed and controlled.

You can often recog   s in activities that you currently enjoy. You may be able to   st part of your work.

Everything included   uilding **(GT)** guide is designed to maximize these char   is sense of *Flow,* because *Flow* represents a state of   Just think of an entire team operating in true *Flow* and maxin   tary individual strengths. The coach's efforts must maintai   can accomplish this task, the team can pretty much take it fi   l sense, you are a *Flow* Coach. The goal of the Guerrilla   de to is help individuals maximize a state of *Flow* in their   ge of the team process.

An effective team wc   members' peak potential. Let's review why this concept is c   ideavors and how the Guerrilla Teambuilding **(GT)** r   .imize *Flow* states in teams. All steps described so far fit nicely with Csikszentmihalyi's parameters for creating *Flow*-based activities. Here's the application spelled out.

- **Make all your component services and / or activities fit together** in a *standardized* manner. This maximizes clarity of task. "I know what to do and how I can easily access what I need as a member of this team." Snap it on — Snap it off! **Building-blocks** and **Visual Operations Plans** = clarity!

- **Discover the skills and preferences of each team member** and develop assignments and roles that meet members' technical and interactional abilities optimally. This will provide appropriate workplace challenges. The team structure leverages your ability to do this by choreographing these optimal strengths. No one works predominantly out of her or his weakest areas, no one works over her or his head and no one works below her or his abilities.

- **Create team structures that transform mundane tasks** into structured goals. Give these "chores" a sense of challenge while adding moment-by-moment feedback on task accomplishment.

- **Create and maintain frequent meetings and open, harmonious communication** to maximize feedback in the often ambiguous and unstructured work environment. There are interactional components to this communication process and there are technologies available that help manage this functional communication. Guerrilla Teambuilding **(GT)** addresses both these important means of maximizing team feedback. Both must be combined to maintain moment-to-moment feedback.

- **Make sure everyone knows other team members and can talk openly** and constructively about differences. This maximizes communication effectiveness and the ability to provide moment-to-moment feedback!

- **Instill processes that minimize drudgery** and distractions while maximizing singular focus. Remember OHIO — Only Handle It Once!

Illustration 9

SLOW TO *FLOW*

SLOW	***SLOW***	***SLOW***	***SLOW***	***SLOW***

Sally was walking a tightrope of unknown demands	Jane was reaching for elusive resources	Bill was stymied by excessive demands	Greg was motionless from lack of direction.	Jeff was crawling through new job responsibilities

FLOW	***FLOW***	***FLOW***	***FLOW***	***FLOW***

Until clear goals allowed her to *Flow!*	Until teaming with knowledgeable peers let her *glide!*	Until pooling resources *lightened* his load!	Until defined responsibilities put some *bounce* in his step!	Until channeling toward his *strengths* got him climbing again!

OTF

OTF is an acronym for OHIO — Team Meeting — *Flow*. Integrating OHIO, Team Structure and Flow is the job of the coach, so OTF is shorthand for "the coach's process model". This Guerrilla Teambuilding **(GT)** guide documents in detail the principles, methods and procedures used to build Guerrilla Teams. How do you build a Guerrilla Team? OTF!

OHIO is the operating premise of the team structure. Guerrilla Teams meet to make *and implement* decisions. They conduct the action necessary to complete the process *right-then-and-there*. This is far better than simple group decision-making with later implementation, which would involve several more steps.

- **Think of an implementation procedure in terms of the physical movement of an object and the action of friction upon it.** An object is pushed into motion. Whether it's on level ground, going downhill, or even going uphill, the forces of gravity and friction will eventually grind it to a halt. With each impact (tiny nudges into other objects, bumps in the road, slowdowns) that the object experiences, there will be a lessening of the initial energy / inertia it had, and the sooner it will come to a halt. The object will require additional energy to get it going again.

- **Think of this process as analogous to a bobsled.** The two-person bobsled team revs up and moves back and forth to gain momentum so that when the starting gun sounds, the team puts as much force into the initial push as possible. You hear the analysts say that this initial push can make or break the entire final time. These athletes train extensively and are highly conditioned just to give this first thirty-second initial push. This initial push is everything, and it has to carry the sled through the entire course. Then, while going down the course at breakneck speed, the sled has to be steered quite precisely, so that it stays in the middle of the track. Every time it veers off center, it encounters friction in the form of tiny impacts that slow the initial push and the ongoing momentum. Because only fractions of seconds can separate first and last place at this championship level, every action that minimizes the initial energy or momentum (causing reduced performance) makes the difference between succeeding and simply finishing the course.

- **Just think what it would be like if you managed all of your team tasks, from the smallest to the largest, as if each one were an Olympic bobsled run**, and each additional and unnecessary step you placed in a procedure was tantamount to adding friction and slowing the momentum of your team in this breakneck competition (see Illustration 10, p. 90). How would this affect your thinking, planning, and implementation practices?

OHIO leads to a team structure that accomplishes tasks immediately. Immediate task accomplishment and minimization of obstacles maximize *Flow*. Creating and maintaining *Flow* provides the team with each individual's best performance on a nearly continuous basis, by leading with each individual's greatest strengths and minimizing individual weaknesses.

Illustration 10

OTF Bobsled

This diagram illustrates the Bobsled analogy of the *Coach* navigating the team through the maze / environment through which the team must pass to achieve the goal. The *Coach* must take caution to guide the team through the tightly woven maze (or course) without hitting the sides of the course — losing speed and momentum, and limiting *Flow*.

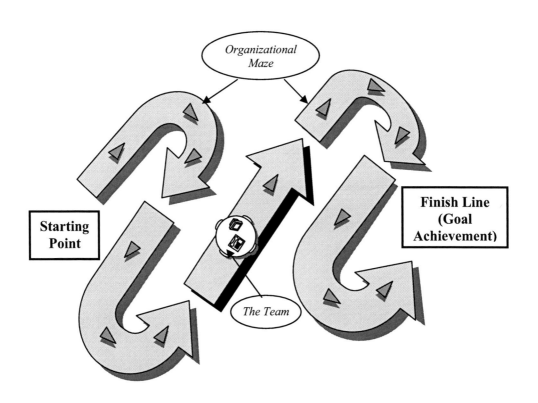

The end result is the creation of "super-workers" and orchestrating the efforts of these "super-workers" creates "super-teams" — that is, teams that can outperform the best individual efforts. Using all of these steps together will outperform the use of any of the steps in isolation.

It is the manager's (coach's) task to:

- **choose team members well** and / or educate members of existing teams as to their best fit, connections, and individual strengths and weaknesses;

- **know oneself** as a manager / coach and how one can best help the team;

- and **make the process happen**.

This is the OHIO — Team Meeting — *Flow*, or OTF model (see Illustration 11, page 92). Look again at the coach's task. *Knowing*, is not enough. Yes, coaches must not only choose and know the team, educate the team, leverage strengths and weaknesses, know themselves and their interface with the team. But they must also create the structures and conditions to set OTF in motion. They must help the team maintain OTF, and get obstacles out of the team's way (behind or in front of the scenes) that interfere with OTF.

As a successful coach, you will need to present the tasks and assignments to the team in a manner that maximizes OTF. This can be emotionally difficult (but the rewards are worth the effort). Even more so than with other team models, over-management can destroy a Guerrilla Team. Consider the following.

- **You manage assignments.** Your efforts should be directed at making them work together as a team. Although you may be able to do some of the tasks they do, perhaps better than the team members (Michael Jordan and Magic Johnson both became coaches — it's a fairly common model), you must stick to making the OTF process happen. This is your first responsibility.

- **You coach,** once the group has been created, educated, and fitted to maintain OTF. When you receive an assignment, you need to tell your Guerrilla Team *what* to do, but *not how* to do it. Don't tell the team how to implement the tasks (Goleman cites compelling research in *Working with Emotional Intelligence* showing that a self-directed team's performance is negatively impacted by this type of supervisory direction). You present the assignment and describe what the team needs to accomplish. You give the team members the parameters of what resources they have at their disposal, and you give time frames and other parameters. The team members will come back to you and show you what they are doing to:
    - o   see if they are achieving the goal;
    - o   see if they are using resources appropriately;
    - o   ask you for more resources;
    - o   ask you to fix things (as only a manager can!) that are impeding their *Flow*;
    - o   and possibly to tap into your expertise (I emphasize *possibly*).

Illustration 11

OTF Management

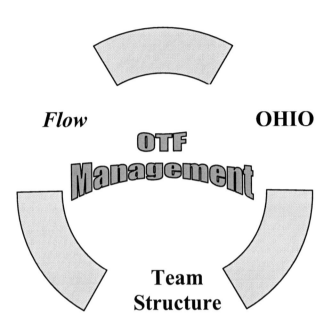

Flow   OHIO

Team
Structure

Flow:	
Peak performance state for team members	**All these elements work together simultaneously and synergistically to form the new gestalt (greater than the sum of its parts) termed OTF Management.**
OHIO:	
Simplify all processes, minimize and combine steps, eliminate duplication of efforts	
Team Structure:	
How, when, and where are meetings held? What are the goals for each meeting? What is accomplished in each meeting? How do team members communicate and coordinate?	

- **You guide.** Because you have some particular expertise in what they are doing, you will want to provide direct input from time to time. I suggest that you ask team members about particular steps they present to you, rather than offer suggestions. It is more appropriate and less *Flow* impacting to give your input this way because it still defines them as the experts. When you want to give suggestions, make sure you have heard them out first and then,

  1. ask them if you can offer some suggestions, and
  2. present any suggestions in terms of, "Have you considered doing this…?" or "Do you think this could work here more effectively…?" or "Do you think this practice would be just as effective, because it would be CHEAPER!"

- **You do NOT mess with success.** You have helped create a well-oiled, finely tuned machine and boosted the sense of self-efficacy, confidence, and morale of every team member. Don't mess with that (that would be an OHIO violation — if done in a frequent and trivial manner) by being overly directive. Let the team members do what they were enlisted to do.

- **You do NOT disengage.** Non-interference does not mean that the coach should never say "no", when you feel it is appropriate. It does not mean that you may not periodically need to "jump in". It certainly does not mean that you have relinquished your ultimate responsibilities. As the leader, you will have to jump in from time to time. The coach must balance the endless ambiguities of knowing when to take the reins and when to relinquish them. In the Guerrilla Teambuilding **(GT)** model, more often than not, you will need to relinquish power related to implementation. But not power related to resource utilization and assigning goals and objectives. You get paid the "big bucks," so you need to deal with the ambiguities and tough decisions. There is no road map for this process. There is coaching, consultation, and contemplation.

This is your mission, if you should choose to accept…. "Good luck, Jim!" (Younger readers, or those who had more constructive things to do with their Saturday nights, will obviously miss the reference to the original — and the BEST — *Mission Impossible* team from the 1960's television series starring Peter Graves. A true Guerrilla Team!)

Illustration 12 (page 94) summarizes the Guerrilla Teambuilding **(GT)** principles. The **(GT)** process model is built upon a foundation of *Knowing* the Team, the Coach and the crucial interactional relationship between these members. Upon this foundation rests a Team Structure, built from optimal task assignments and meeting practices. Guerrilla Team functions are consistently conducted based upon the guiding OHIO standard. The result is *Flow*, the exceptionally productive operating state of a Guerilla Team!

Illustration 12

Guerrilla Teambuilding Hierarchy

- Foundation pieces define relationships and human capital (resources & skills).

- Team Structures are created based upon interactional and skill knowledge.

- OHIO maximizes efficiency of team structures.

- *Flow* is the peak performance state created from these first three building-blocks.

- OTF Management is the process of building the steps to *Flow* and maintaining *Flow*.

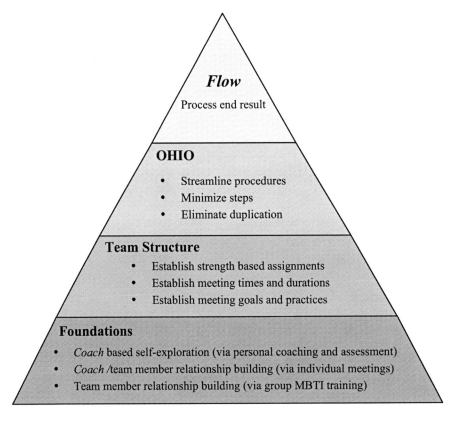

Flow
Process end result

OHIO
- Streamline procedures
- Minimize steps
- Eliminate duplication

Team Structure
- Establish strength based assignments
- Establish meeting times and durations
- Establish meeting goals and practices

Foundations
- *Coach* based self-exploration (via personal coaching and assessment)
- *Coach* /team member relationship building (via individual meetings)
- Team member relationship building (via group MBTI training)

The Guerrilla Teambuilding **(GT)** guide serves as a tool for use in implementing successful coaching endeavors. It presents proven guidelines, techniques, methods, procedures and parameters that you can use. The coach has a tough job! Tools like **(GT)** can help. When you undertake this Guerrilla Teambuilding (GT) process, there is more help available. Additional related materials, advice, support and consultation are available through the J. F. Zagotta & Associates, LLC website (www.jfzassoc.com). Please feel free to visit, seek assistance, or at least let us know how your Guerrilla Team is doing!

Implementation Checklists 5 through 7 are provided on the next three pages. These should be used as a basis for team discussion, as the next steps toward implementing **(GT)** within your organization.

Implementation Checklist 5

OHIO

- How does your organization currently make decisions?

- Does your organization and / or team repeat their efforts? Frequently? How?

- Do team meetings and structures repeat efforts?

- Do team members and / or the organization find that they repeatedly confront the same issues and the same decisions over and over?

- What are the strengths of your organization's decision-making processes?

- Conduct a review of your team meeting to look for, strengthen, and implement the OHIO standard within the task implementation and decision-making process.

- Do the various steps or procedures within your organization, department, or team-structure duplicate effort or require unnecessary waiting for materials and / or decisions that are beyond the team's control?

Notes:

Implementation Checklist 6

Flow

- Do your team members know their responsibilities, tasks, and procedures?

- Do team members have clearly defined roles?

- Do the team members have assignments that match their ability levels optimally (not too challenging, not too easy)?

- Are drudgery assignments turned into activities with moment-to-moment monitoring and clear goals, accomplished within a group format to lessen their negative impact?

- Do your processes, team meetings, and team functions involve moment-to-moment feedback? What feedback intervals are present?

- How can team functions maximize feedback intervals?

- How can communication skills and technological tools maximize team members' ability to give feedback to each other, as well as improve the greater organization's ability to give feedback to the team?

- Have you minimized distractions and / or unnecessary interruptions to team meetings and to *Flow* activities for the team members?

Notes:

Implementation Checklist 7

Coaching the Team

- As the coach, do you understand how OHIO, Team Structure, and *Flow* are culminating in your team effectiveness?

- Can you articulate how OTF is maximized within your team?

- Can the team articulate how OTF is maximized within the team?

- Initiate regular discussions within team meetings about the maximization of OTF integration and functioning.

- Seek feedback from the team members about how you, as the coach, can protect them from issues within the organization that negatively affect *Flow* and / or OTF functioning.

- Identify your current strengths in routing and organizing resources for your team that maximize *Flow* and OTF functioning.

- Review and seek feedback from the team as to what additional steps you could take to maximize *Flow* and OTF functioning.

Notes:

Chapter Seven

Guerrilla Team Case Study

"The Starship Enterprise"

Guerrilla Team Models

There are many actual life models of true Guerrilla Teams. But there are also fictional models of such teams in movies, literature, and television.

- **These fictional models provide a frame of reference** to which many of us can relate. We know the characters, their strengths, their weaknesses and the way they work together. And we remember their mission assignments and outcomes.

- **Sometimes these are better than real life** examples because of these common reference points.

With these considerations in mind, we will examine an iconic Guerrilla Team to model the principles of this guide.

The Crew of the Starship Enterprise

In the glory days of television (at least in my opinion), this original 1960's science fiction, action-adventure series starred William Shatner, Leonard Nimoy, DeForest Kelly, James Doohan, Nichelle Nichols, Walter Koenig and George Takei.

Let's take a closer look at how this group of individuals embodied the concepts found in this guide. First, let's review the well-defined *Strengths* and *Challenges* embodied in these classic characterizations.

Kirk:

Strengths
- The overview person / problem solver.
- The best at taking in data (not obtaining it himself) and sorting it into an effective "gut" feeling and course of action.
- The face of the group to the world. At ease and confident in social or negotiating situations. Strong inspiring leader – charismatic.
- Strong with the *big picture*.
- Most effective with a team backing him up. Highly effective with supportive players.

Challenges
- He can be *so* charming that, at times, it distracts and gets him into trouble!
- Not the person to acquire facts. Not strong on details or the mundane.

Spock:

Strengths

- The quintessential analyst.
- The greatest backup in the galaxy.
- The best in a crisis. Cool as a cucumber.
- Objective and a wealth of information.
- An unbeatable pair with Kirk (Mr. Outer World and Mr. Inner World; Mr. Integration and Mr. Sensory Input). As symbiotic a pair as is possible!

Challenges

- Poor impact on morale.
- Stifles emotional reactions.
- Insults and offends others unknowingly.
- At times, he has a highly negative impact on team harmony.

Uhura:

Strengths

- The most well-rounded member of the crew.
- Not many extremes in her profile. Hence, she lacks the outright strengths of a Kirk, but possesses the greatest ability to "do it all."
- The glue and compassion of the team.
- Trust and nurturing to the outside world.
- A superstar of balance and multi-tasking. The ability to bring people and cultures together.

Challenges

- Limited overt challenging areas, apart from the acceptable limitations that come from being well balanced.

Chekhov:

Strengths

- Passionate and vibrant. Youthful curiosity.
- His exuberance and cute boyishness bring harmony to the team.
- You feel good around him and absorb some of his energy.
- He has some basic technical / interpersonal skills, but his strengths to the team are in motivational and emotional tone.

Challenges

- He makes the mistakes of the novice, of youth, and of impulsivity.
- Like others with this affliction, he does not have great insight into the fact that he does this or behaves this way.
- He must be paired with a seasoned pro to provide balance!

Bones:

Strengths
- The ultimate nurturer, questioner and advocate.
- A source of emotions and feelings in a mechanized world.
- The strength of old school relationships.
- A conscience to the team's calculated and objective thought.
- Technical expertise combined with the best of emotion and conscience.

Challenges
- Leads with the heart, can be too emotional, sometimes to the point of inaction.
- Not as vital in the physical sense (can't really "kick ass" like the rest of the crew).

Sulu:

Strengths
- Physically strong, focused and unrelenting.
- Implementation is reflexive.
- Knows the rules and how to implement them.
- Dependable, skilled, disciplined both physically and mentally.
- Respectful. Others feel safe around him and find comfort in his strength.
- The mature confidence of physical prowess.
- The protector – he was the chief of security.

Challenges
- Not as in tune with the emotional world and not an emotional leader.
- When the extremes come out, he may come across as ruthless and / or uncaring.

Scotty:

Strengths
- The details / technical guy who integrates technology into the team.
- His technology maintained Flow: "I need more power, Scotty."
- He organizes the physical world for the group.
- He brings a personal and supportive face to technology.
- He does this in an almost nurturing way.
- He is fun to be around and has supportive and comforting emotional energy.

Challenges
- He can be overcome by his emotions and can be quite a hothead at times.
- Sometimes cannot see the forest for the trees. Can be a rigid and / or inflexible thinker.

Figure 11

Enterprise Crew — MBTI Types

An overview of each Start Trek crew member's *assumed* MBTI type appears in the following table.

Crew Member	Type	Strengths	Challenges
Kirk	ENFP	Outgoing, Charismatic, Adventurous, Open to Possibilities.	Romantic Distractions, Always Exploring.
Spock	ISTJ	Focused, Keeps Others On Track, Calm, Collected.	Analytical, Objective, Perceived Insensitive, Impact on Morale.
Uhura	ESFJ	Brings Others Together, Reads Others Well, Supportive, Positive Morale Builder, Structured.	Could be a Bigger Risk Taker. Limitations of Balance.
Bones	ESFP	Fun Loving, Passionate, Supportive, Divergent Thinker, Advocate.	Overly Emotional, Overly Critical, Self-Righteous.
Sulu	ISTJ	Focused, Fair, Structured, Dependable.	Less In-Tune with Emotional Aspects, Periodically Portrayed a Ruthless Side.
Chekhov	ENFP	Passionate, Novice, Curiosity, Sensitive, Supportive, Willing.	Leaps-Before-Looks, Impulsive, Emotional.
Scottie	ESFJ	Personable, Objective, Factual, Supportive, Sensitive, Problem Solver.	Prone to Inflexible, Non-Divergent Thinking, Can be a "Hot-Head."

All of these character types should sound familiar.

- You interact with them, or various composites of them, every day. Their strengths, foibles and differences should be recognizable in the people you see daily (including yourself).

- When you examine the cohesive unit they formed and view their function as a team, do you have any doubt they could take on the Klingon Empire; a 2000 kilometer single cell organism; a group of green vestal virgins; or a personality altering virus within the crew?

- Nothing could stop these people, and it is absolutely understandable because they were the ultimate team. My premise is that you, too, can create (to some extent) this same team effectiveness.

Let's look closer at what made them so effective and why they were one of the ultimate Guerrilla Teams!

Team Structure and Leveraging Diversity

- **The members of the team all have their particular strengths.** They were well suited to each other in their strengths and in their types (basically). The assignments given to each represented a personal strength, and members' assignments and strengths did not overlap excessively.

- **Kirk, Spock and Sulu could "kick ass."** You didn't see them send in Bones for hand-to-hand combat with the invading Klingons. The medical officer, when allowed to set up his own mobile lab, often saved the day with what he discovered. This usually occurred while Kirk and Spock were out beating people up to ensure that Bones could do his job uninterrupted. In other cases, Kirk, Spock and Sulu would "kick ass" when there were invaders on the ship, which allowed Uhuru to fix the communications equipment and contact Star Fleet to send help.

- **They knew their roles, they knew their strengths and they knew how to deploy these skills very quickly.** Being no expert, I believe this is a general strength in military structures — including *Star Fleet*.

- **Note that their strengths were not only specialized training or technical expertise**. Their areas of technical expertise complemented the people they were. **Kirk** was the extrovert and was a good lead to send in when negotiating with others. He had a commanding presence, and the galaxy usually paid attention to him. **Uhuru** was an effective communicator and interpreter of culture. The connections she saw often aided the team to reach out and bring together various forces of the galaxy and the entities they encountered. Building alliances was important, and she made the team effective at it. **Sulu's** order and structure and his knowledge of the martial arts made him a strong security officer. He was dependable and reliable; he could implement his assignments, and he made the ship safe. **Chekhov** was more supportive and an emotional energy provider. He was young and foolhardy, but he brought exuberance for the job and an emotional tone that catalyzed the effectiveness of the team. **Scotty** also brought energy, both in anti-matter propulsion and emotional forms. He made sure that technology worked and provided a nice balance of passion and skills. **Spock** would think things through, was a walking encyclopedia – sometimes better than the computer – and was often the quintessential crisis responder. **Bones** contributed joviality and passion to the team.

- **In the barbs between Spock and Bones, we saw an antagonism that brought out the best of the thinking and the feeling worlds.** Both were better together than they were in isolation, and the team was better off because of this spirited antagonism. They both held technical and interpersonal strengths and relied upon their *collective* strengths to accomplish goals. Although crew members had their various cultural differences, they were able to leverage the strengths of these cultural differences and stay in *Flow*.

OTF management

- **They were masters of "OHIO."** The beauty of the show as an example of implementing the Guerrilla Team model was that it lasted only one hour. There wasn't time for unnecessary deliberation — if you deliberated too long, you died!

- **Their meetings lasted indefinitely** in that they were all housed on the bridge of the ship together and had a perpetual office in place. Their sensors gave them constant feedback from the outside and on their mission. They systemically used technology to help maintain a *Flow* state. They had immediate communication with team members, whether in close proximity or far away. If you recognize the bridge as one continuous team meeting, then they certainly did things *right-then-and-there.*

- **Everything they did was decisive, goal directed, done in proximity** and in harmony with one another (even when they were irritated at each other). They were action oriented: they didn't just talk, they acted! They lived the 8 elements of *Flow*. They knew their jobs, achieved moment-to-moment feedback and were assigned at an optimal skill level.

- **Their coach led in such a way that he did not micro-manage**. He utilized the self-directed team to its utmost potential.

- **The "One-Hour Snapshot."** Maybe we could all learn something from this time parameter. It certainly seemed to help focus this team.

Why the Crew of the Enterprise was a True Guerrilla Team

Top Twenty Reasons

1. All the members knew themselves, and their leader knew them.

2. Their leader did not micromanage them but implicitly relied on their skills as professionals and people.

3. Their leader put tasks before them ("give me more power") and let them execute their missions as they saw fit.

4. They could discuss their weaknesses, foibles, and differences openly. They would bring these into discussions / disagreements, and they could laugh at them. (They would end every life-threatening, galaxy-ending peril with a final episode joke, usually focusing on a comical aspect of their differences.)

5. They maximally leveraged their individual strengths, skills and knowledge bases. Each team member was allowed to lead with her or his strengths.

6. #5 again.

7. #5 again (number 5 is important)!

8. They supported one another, and watched one another's backs to negate their weaknesses.

9. They leveraged the strengths of their diversity.

10. #9 again.

11. #9 again (number 9 is important)!

12. By relying on each team member's identified strengths, they minimized the drudgery of people leading with their weaknesses and maximized team *Flow*.

13. With their combined strengths, they were a formidable opponent to any force in the galaxy, no matter what God-like powers other species possessed.

14. They seldom, if ever, came across others who were as effective a team as they were. That's why they always won!

15. They were highly emotionally intelligent and usually left even their opponents feeling good about losing to them.

    Note: *While this exact topic (Emotional Intelligence) may be less of a focus in this guide, it certainly warrants study for its positive impact on team effectiveness.*

16. They instantly accomplished tasks as they talked about them. They did not wait a week or send something to committee. They minimized the process steps. Consider this small example of a hypothetical team meeting on the bridge:
    Kirk: "What is the big blob made of?"
    Crew input: "It's like a human beta killer cell."

Kirk:	"How do you disable a human beta killer cell?"
Crew Input:	"With protoxin neutrino C."
Kirk:	"Bones, immediately make some protoxin neutrino C to disable the blob. *[Not kill: remember the emotionally intelligent prime directive – it was a good business model.]* Scottie, give me more power to the engines and keep this thing from sucking us in. Spock, figure out a way to shoot the protoxin neutrino C into this blob. Uhura, see if you can communicate with this thing and get it to back off while we are working on this. Chekhov and Sulu, keep the ship straight so that it doesn't suck us in."

Now that's OHIO!

17. They used technology to make accomplishing tasks more effective, more efficient, and less mundane. In doing so, they maximized *Flow*. They integrated technology; they did not use it as something to go to but as the way they did things, again maximizing *Flow*.

18. They had fun! Their tasks left them in physical proximity, and their meeting structures were effective, while promoting a sense of team or *esprit de corps*!

19. They were more than the sum of their parts.

20. They never lost track of the team process as the central tool for accomplishing their goals!

Hail the crew of the Starship Enterprise – a true Guerrilla Team!

Final thoughts on Implementing Guerrilla Teambuilding (GT)

Can you be as effective as the *Enterprise* crew?

- **Yes, you can.** Or you can at least approximate that effectiveness and accomplish some incredible things by utilizing the steps of this program.

- **Basic informational tools.** Many of the basic ideas found in this guide are expanded upon and supported, including original research and great detail, in the following sources:

  A. Daniel Goleman et al., *Emotional Intelligence, Working with Emotional Intelligence, Primal Leadership*

  B. Mihaly Csikszenymihalyi, *Flow*

  C. Isabel Briggs Myers, *Introduction to Type*.

  These and other sources of information are listed as full citations in **References**, page 124, for the reader's convenience. I encourage you to explore these resources as supports in implementing this program.

- *Live Long and Prosper!* The guidelines presented may not exactly make your team the crew of the *Enterprise*, but they will certainly help you overcome a *tribble* or two.

A last request – let us know how your Guerrilla Team is doing. You can always contact us at www.jfzassoc.com.

Appendix A

Myers Briggs Type Indicator

MBTI Overview

The MBTI, an assessment tool developed by the mother-daughter team of Isabel Briggs Myers and Katherine Myers, is based upon the psychological theories of the Swiss psychoanalyst Carl Gustav Jung, a student of Freud's and a member of Freud's inner circle. Jung went on to develop his own unique psychoanalytically based theory. A wonderful overview on the MBTI instrument, presented in a brief and easy-to-read visually-based format, is found in Isabel Briggs Meyers' *Introduction to Type* (1998, Consulting Psychologists Press, Inc.). Presented in a small manual format, it is available through the CPP website (www.cpp.com). For those who wish to learn more about *Type* and the many useful applications of the MBTI, CPP offers additional invaluable resources for this task.

Jung and the MBTI

The following is a very brief review of Jung's theory as it relates to the MBTI development. Central to Jung's theory was his premise that people have dualities of the characteristics they display to the outside world. These dualities typically form polar opposites that serve as different ends of a continuum. Further, all individuals have dominant modes. These dominant modes are *preferences* for which end of a continuum they display to the outer world. All people have abilities and characteristics across the continuum but actually *prefer* one end that they exhibit or operate from with greatest ease. These preferences or "dominant functions," as Jung put it, combine to form personality constructs and predictabilities / generalities of functioning. Jung was the original user of the terms *introversion* and *extroversion*. His concepts related to manifest and latent personality functioning have become embedded in much of our understanding of psychodynamic thinking.

Jung described that the active mind is involved in two basic activities: *perceiving* (the process of acquiring information) and *judging* (structuring information in order to form opinions or make decisions). He further described that people have two opposite ways to perceive: *sensation* (details) and *intuition* (constructs). And people have two opposite ways to judge or make decisions: *thinking* (objectivity) and *feeling* (subjectivity). Jung also described that people can focus their energies and / or attention on the outer-world, termed *extroversion* (which can include, but is not limited to, people, experiences, activities, and general social stimulation), or on the inner-world, referred to as *introversion* (which can include, but is not limited to, ideas, memories, and thoughts). These are the key building-blocks that comprise the MBTI. Myers and Briggs took these building-blocks, and then reformulated and expanded the theory into the basic format presented in Figure 12 (on the following page).

Figure 12

Overview of MBTI dichotomies

One can predominantly focus one's *mental energy* on:

The Outer-World   ←——————→   The Inner-World
Extroversion   *Introversion*

One can predominantly *take in information*:

That is real, tangible, actual, or   That is connection or "the big
and detail oriented   ←——————→   picture" oriented
Sensing   *Intuition*

One can predominantly organize thoughts and / or *make decisions* based on:

Analyzing pros & cons and   Identifying with others and
utilizing objective standards   ←——————→   what is important to "them"
Thinking   *Feeling*

One can predominantly *deal with the outer world* by:

Using planned, ordered, and   Using flexible, spontaneous,
predictable ways   ←——————→   and "take it as it comes" ways
Judging   *Perceiving*

Figure 13

The 16 MBTI Type Combinations

Remember that:

E = Extroversion	**I = Introversion**
S = Sensing	**N = Intuitive**
T = Thinking	**F = Feeling**
J = Judging	**P = Perceiving**

The 16 Type combinations are:

ISTJ	**ISFJ**	**INFJ**	**INTJ**
ISTP	**ISFP**	**INFP**	**INTP**
ESTP	**ESFP**	**ENFP**	**ENTP**
ESTJ	**ESFJ**	**ENFJ**	**ENTJ**

MBTI Interpretation

The use and interpretation of the MBTI instrument and individual results becomes complicated and sophisticated when examining an individual's dominant and / or less dominant preferences. This presentation provides an adequate but not in-depth discussion of these concepts. When taking the MBTI, individual responses are matched statistically with other responders, representing known *Types*, which comprise a normative comparison group. This provides results that measure the degree to which the responder matches a preference factor along each continuum. For each factor, the results may be somewhere in the middle or very clearly at one end of the continuum. MBTI results should not be accepted conclusively, but validated through a process of exploration with the individual. The accuracy of results is reviewed with the responder, and the original *Type* profile is then modified or accepted, based on this validation. The use of qualified professionals is crucial to using these tools appropriately and providing an enriching and rewarding assessment experience. This is also why (in my opinion) face-to-face interpretation of MBTI results is an essential part of the overall process.

The dominant preferences are often explained through parallels to the concept of "handedness." When you operate out of your non-dominant preferences, it feels akin to writing with your non-dominant hand. You can physically do this, but it takes a great deal of effort, and you'd rather be using your dominant hand. (Think about how that would affect team *Flow*.) If you prefer examining details, you may be challenged by the big picture. If you gain your energy through introspection, you may be challenged by the public spotlight. These are all okay and not more or less appropriate than being right- or left-handed. It's all about fit, compensation, adaptation, and the need to strengthen skills that you rely upon less often. The MBTI instrument yields a matrix of 16 possible *Type* combinations. Figure 13 (on the previous page) summarizes this matrix.

MBTI Limitations

Type combination is not an exhaustive explanation of any individual's personality make-up or functioning. But it provides useful insights into social and interactional strengths and "fits" that correspond to an individual's "dominant" preferences. Beyond an overview of the characteristics associated with each preference continuum, I will not provide further elaboration on the functional implications for each *Type*. The reader is again referred to the CPP website (www.cpp.com) for a wealth of additional material. The reader is also encouraged to seek a qualified professional to receive individual, couple, or team-based MBTI results within the context of a general growth and understanding process or for a more applied application such as teambuilding or career enrichment.

The MBTI has proven itself to be an invaluable tool in helping individuals, couples, and teams to understand differences respectfully. It accomplishes these goals in validating, supportive, and non-villainizing ways; it assists in leveraging areas of strength; and it develops affirming learning plans to compensate for and address areas of challenge. The instrument's developers deeply believed in the MBTI's ability to promote positive understanding between people from highly diverse backgrounds. Few tools, psychometric or otherwise, have been as effective towards accomplishing this goal as the MBTI.

Appendix B

Coaching

Coaching Overview

Coaching has come to mean a range of services that focus on assisting individuals and organizations to achieve specific goals through supportive interaction, collaborative discussion, and problem solving activities. This field of endeavor is not historically new, but it has been recently popularized. The scope has broadened to include personal goals and other non-traditional areas that many would typically not have viewed as amenable to a coaching application. The goals and practice are not exceptionally different from the traditional usage in sports, personal training, or dietary / nutritional applications, where these have been accepted services used for many years. The personal coaching movement is a more recent development, not quite as established as its organizational / business consulting counterpart.

Coaching, in its current popular form, seeks to assist individuals and groups in moving towards a skill acquisition or goals that a client has set. While the coach may possess particular educational or technical expertise in specific areas, the key to the coach's role is assisting the client to establish, move towards, and achieve a goal. This is where the coach's true expertise emerges. The coach's ultimate effectiveness need not rest with technical expertise in a given area, but rather in the ability to assist individuals and organizations in moving towards their chosen goals.

Coaching differs from traditional "therapy" services in several key ways. In coaching, the focus rests on the here-and-now and the future. Past determinants of behaviors are not the area of focus. With Coaching, the client is seeking services from a perspective of "health" and proactive life advancement. Also, no model or paradigm for client "pathology" or "illness" exists within the coaching framework. While traditional therapeutic skills such as empathy, emotional support, and proactive listening are strong components of the effective coach's repertoire, therapeutic techniques focusing on past insight and other dramatic methods of promoting behavior change are not applicable. A Coach must have strong interactive skills but need not be a trained "therapist". Indeed, many professionals approaching coaching from more traditional psychotherapeutic backgrounds will require additional training to achieve this shift of focus.

Coaching-Related Organizations

Relatively few formalized training programs exist for this specialty, so consumers should be cautious of the background, skills, and qualifications of those presenting themselves as professional coaches. In attempts to regulate and offer a higher degree of consumer confidence, several organizations have developed professional standards and certification for individuals delivering services termed "coaching."

The largest such organization, the International Coaching Federation (ICF) (www.coachfederation.org), has attempted to establish standards and regulate services provided under the coaching title. Another organization, the Professional Coaching and Mentors Association (PCMA) (pcmaonline.com), focuses more specifically on business professionals and organizations. The PCMA's activities encompass both formal and informal processes through which professional development occurs in an organizational setting. I encourage the reader to visit both websites to learn more about the coaching process and these organizations.

I have personally received coach training from the "College of Executive Coaching" (CEC). I needed to learn how to make the transition from therapist to coach. Training behavioral health professionals in this type of transition is the CEC's specialty. The CEC was founded and is headed by Jeffrey Auerbach, Ph.D. Dr. Auerbach is a clinical psychologist who transferred his clinical practice into the coaching / consulting arena, where he has now practiced for many years. He has developed an effective coach training model aimed at professionals who hold advanced degrees in the mental / behavioral health arenas (as well as other advanced specialty areas), and who seek to transition to a coaching / consulting based practice. The program is uniquely suited for doctoral level psychologists making this change and maximizes the strengths they have to bring to this endeavor. The majority of the faculty at the CEC are doctoral psychologists who have transitioned into or have worked throughout their careers in the coaching / consulting field.

I encourage the reader to visit the CEC website (www.executivecoachcollege.com) to learn more about this organization, its training programs, and the other professional services offered by the college. Dr. Auerbach has authored a very useful introductory book on understanding the coaching process entitled *Personal and Executive Coaching*. The book is geared towards behavioral health professionals seeking to transition or diversify into a coaching-based practice and also offers a wealth of general information related to professional coaching and consultation services. The book can be purchased from the CEC website.

Two larger training and consulting groups worth mentioning as leaders in the arena of business / organizational coaching / consulting are The Center for Creative Leadership (CCL), and RHR International. The Center for Creative Leadership (www.ccl.org) is involved in research and the coaching / training of business leaders, including many Fortune 500 company executives. The Center has an international reputation for assisting in the development of highly effective managerial professionals and serving as a world-class coaching and research institution. Several of the CEC faculty have direct affiliation with the CCL. Visit the CCL's website to learn more about this organization and the many open enrollment leadership training programs they offer. The RHR organization (www.rhrinternational.com), is a well-established and predominantly psychologically-focused organizational consulting group. A wealth of information related to this aspect of professional coaching can be found at their website.

Appendix C

Assessment Tools

The MBTI

The Myers-Briggs Type Indicator is possibly the most widely used psychometric inventory within organizational and career counseling environments. In use for over five decades, it has extensive research support and cross-cultural validation. Exploring the strengths, preferences, and interactive styles of the various MBTI *Types* has proven rewarding for thousands within the organizational training and career counseling arenas. Extensive volumes have been written on the value of *Type* exploration. The literature is too vast to adequately cover here. A nice review of the benefits of using *Type* in the career enrichment process is found in Paul D. Treiger's and Barbara Barron-Treiger's book *Do What You Are*, 3rd edition (Little, Brown, 2001). The book provides a basic understanding of Type and its usefulness in an easy to utilize format. I recommend, however, that the reader go on to actually take the inventory and have the results interpreted by a qualified professional, as a more fulfilling exploration of this area. *Type* assessment through the MBTI is one of the most basic exploration tools in coaching and teambuilding activities and is often the entry point for assisting clients with their career based goals.

The MBTI is offered by the Consulting Psychologists Press (www.cpp.com). The CPP website contains a wealth of information and offers many products that can help readers familiarize themselves with the concepts underlying *Type* and the MBTI. The MBTI itself can only be purchased through, and administered by, qualified professionals (of which the website also provides listings).

The other inventories presented in this section are useful and are highly recommended, but they are not essential. This is not the case for the MBTI. The strength of MBTI is its ability to provide a common language for discussing differences and preferences in a manner that promotes interpersonal insight, understanding and acceptance of those differences. This tool is crucial to the Guerrilla Teambuilding **(GT)** model. The MBTI is easily accessible, it's not expensive, and neither is individual or group based interpretation and feedback.

The Strong Interest Inventory

The Strong Interest Inventory® is also a well-established and extensively researched assessment tool utilized by thousands in the career selection and enrichment process. (Strong Interest Inventory is a registered trademark of CPP, Inc.) The Strong Inventory is often used in conjunction with the MBTI as a powerful combination to assess career fit and interest.

The MBTI looks at *Type* preferences related to interaction styles, information gathering styles, cognitive processes, and structural or organizational styles. The Strong psychometrically compares an individual's interest in various work based activities with those of other individuals satisfactorily employed in specific career endeavors. This combination can assess and compare an individual's personal style preferences with her or his preferences across well-established career activities and prove a valuable individually- and organizationally-based career building tool.

The Strong is also offered by the Consulting Psychologists Press (www.cpp.com) and has similar qualified user requirements. Qualified professionals can offer this tool to clients in an online format as well, either to be used separately or in special combination packages with the MBTI

Emotional Intelligence and EI Inventories

A brief discussion of the topic of Emotional Intelligence (EI) will prove useful as an introduction to specific EI inventories. EI competencies represent behaviors so fundamental to successful team functioning that their promotion and enhancement cannot be ignored in the teambuilding process, whether or not specific EI inventories are utilized within your Guerrilla program.

The concept that other factors besides IQ play a crucial role in determining an individual's success and satisfaction with career pursuits has been put forward by many, but the concept has largely been popularized by Daniel Goleman in *Emotional Intelligence* (Bantam Books, 1995), and in the subsequent titles *Working With Emotional Intelligence* (Bantam Books, 1998), and *Primal Leadership* (Harvard Business School Press, 2002). Goleman has indicated in subsequent writings that he started the Emotional Intelligence project in response to another popular book of the time, *The Bell Curve* (Richard J. Herrnstein & Charles Murray, Free Press paperbacks, 1994), which made the case for IQ being a prominent factor in determining success across many key functioning areas and suggested that majority groups in the United States had a competitive advantage related to possessing superior IQ scores. IQ, as it turns out, is actually a very poor predictor of career and other areas of success. Numerous studies have pointed out that peak performers in the world of business possess other core, emotionally related competencies including self-awareness, empathy, self-control, and social skills such as influence and team-building. Goleman presents overwhelming research that advanced degrees, technical training, and general intellectual abilities are traditional entry level requirements, but that it is actually these emotionally-based skills that predict success in today's career environment — that these are the factors that predict the "star" career performers and accurately define the vast majority of those who rise to the highest levels of organizational leadership.

In *Working with Emotional Intelligence*, Goleman, a Harvard educated psychologist and experienced scientific journalist, documents that when determining "star" performance in nearly every field of career endeavor, emotional intelligence competencies matter twice as much as cognitive abilities (such as those measured by

IQ) and / or technical expertise. These crucial skills can also be learned, unlike many factors measured by IQ.

Peter Salovey (Yale University) and John Mayer (University of New Hampshire) are psychologists who have pioneered the theory of emotional intelligence and have researched the area extensively. Salovey and Mayer have developed several well-researched and extensively tested measures to assess practical abilities across emotional intelligence areas. The most recent version, the MSCEIT, is available to qualified purchasers (individuals with advanced training in psychometric testing) through Multi Health Systems (www.mhs.com). Reuven Bar-On is another psychologist who has conducted extensive research in this area and who has developed his own self-report measure of emotional intelligence, the Bar-On Emotional Quotient Inventory (EQ-i). Goleman's own research endeavors have led to his development of an additional workplace related emotional intelligence measure, the Emotional Competence Inventory, that relies upon feedback from the individual participant, her or his immediate supervisor, those who report directly to this individual, and the individual's colleagues or same-level peers. Goleman advocates the use of this multi-level assessment approach (termed a 360 evaluation — related to a comprehensive and complete or 360 degree data collection process) as preferable to self-report data alone. All of these measures are widely used in businesses and organizations to assess and strengthen the essential core competencies of emotional intelligence. All authors would advise caution in the process of using these competency assessments and explain that specific care and respect are required when delivering feedback to individuals as well as in preserving the confidentiality of this data within an organizational setting. Publishers of these testing materials advocate for the ethical and appropriate usage of these instruments by trained and qualified professionals who abide by the standards set forth by the American Psychological Association (www.APA.org) in the use of these instruments and in the presentation of assessment results.

Leadership Style Inventories and 360 degree assessments

Current literature is directly indicative of a distinct overlap between leadership success and emotional intelligence competencies. In today's career environment, leadership competencies must be broad, and effective leaders must be able to call upon various styles and skills at the right time, based upon the specific leadership tasks and challenges they face. There are a wide variety of assessment instruments to choose from in this area. Included are those that compare an individual's leadership styles with successful Fortune 500 business leaders as well as those that draw on data in a 360 degree format, using feedback from direct reports, peers, and supervisors (offered to qualified professionals through Consulting Psychologists Press, Inc. — www.cpp.com, The Center for Creative Leadership — www.ccl.org, and other assessment organizations). These tools are specifically applicable to the "coaching the coach" process but may prove useful for individual team members as well. All members of a team assume some leadership roles, and often a team consists of those who are members in one set of teams and coaches in others.

Appendix D

Kaizen Application

Original Sources

Original sources can be found for the foundation ideas behind Kaizen in the writings of W. E. Deming, the American who brought these ideas to Japan, and initiated the subsequent manufacturing revolution in this country. A good overview of this topic is presented in Aguayo's book *Dr. Deming : the American who Taught the Japanese Quality* (1990). Masaaki Imai is the individual who coined the term Kaizen, and the founder of the Kaizen Institute. My brief discussion of the topic is drawn from my experiences on the Diamond Star Motors project, as well as from a review of his books *Kaizen: the Key to Japan's Competitive Success* (1930, 1986), and *Gemba Kaizen : A Commonsense, Low-Cost Approach to Management* (1997). Both books, and the term Kaizen are registered trademarks of the Kaizen Institute. The institute has many international branches that foster the teachings and practices found in these texts. I originally learned of this topic as part of the Diamond Star Motors project, in my supervision from and exposure to senior staff of the HR consulting firm Towers, Perrin, Forester & Crosby (TPF&C). This review presents a "watered-down" and very basic version of Kaizen application, drawn from both formal review and practical experience. The reader is referred to the sources above for information beyond this introductory presentation.

Kaizen Process Components

There are many components to this process. For the purposes of our brief discussion, I will talk about only four: three that are commonly associated with Kaizen, and one additional component of my own invention.

1. Standardization

All workers are cross-trained in a wide variety of positions used at a work site. This allows for interchangeability of personnel. Processes are also standardized and broken down into component functions to ensure ease of staff training and personnel substitution on these interchangeable assignments.

2. Improvement Discussions

Regular, scheduled discussions occur frequently regarding improving the efficiency, effectiveness and quality of the work process. These discussions include optimizing a workers ability to perform a process, and the ease, comfort and safety with which it can be done. All parties' roles in the process are reviewed, reformulated, improved and standardized. These meetings are about outcomes and practical applications. They are highly focused, and drive toward tangible improvements.

3. Safety and Work Environment Issues

During these discussions, not only the quality, efficiency, and effectiveness of the process are reviewed, but a high emphasis is placed upon problem-solving to make the workplace safer. A focus on the quality of the working environment for each individual, and the group as a whole is a key part of ensuring this safety. All parties' responsibilities to ensure the agreed upon decisions are again standardized. Meetings create tangible and measurable results.

4. Synergy (*this is my addition*)

The focus upon interchangeability allows each team member to contribute to performance improvement discussions more effectively, and to help in a rapid response manner if problems of work flow or worker support are identified via the Kaizen productivity and safety discussions. Interchangeability promotes effective worker problem-solving. Effective problem-solving initiation is enhanced by team members' interchangeability and system interchangeability. The more standardized the system, the easier it is to bring resources to address a short fall or other issues (possibly a 1/5 loss in productivity, or a chance to make a 1/5 productivity gain, or a chance to lessen "burnout" or accidents by 1/5 — remember the action trigger topic). Illustration 13 (on the following page) outlines the synergistic effect of this Kaizen type process.

Illustration 13

Kaizen Synergistic Effect

- Component pieces work in a harmonious or synchronized manner.

- Each piece builds upon the presence of the others.

- The component pieces combine together to form a process greater than the sum of its parts.

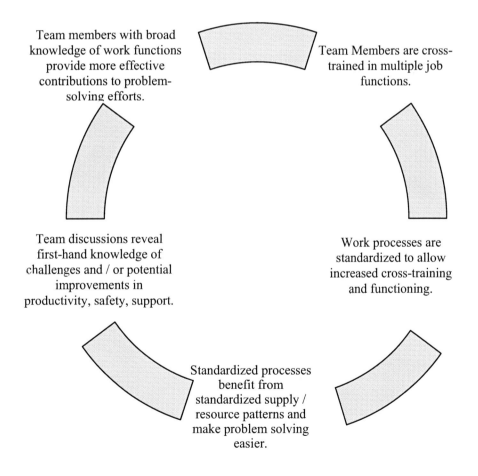

Team members with broad knowledge of work functions provide more effective contributions to problem-solving efforts.

Team Members are cross-trained in multiple job functions.

Team discussions reveal first-hand knowledge of challenges and / or potential improvements in productivity, safety, support.

Work processes are standardized to allow increased cross-training and functioning.

Standardized processes benefit from standardized supply / resource patterns and make problem solving easier.

A Closing Note on Kaizen and the (GT) Program

The Kaizen practices are highly compatible with the Guerilla Teambuilding **(GT)** program in many key ways, although some differences must be accounted for. Similarities abound in the team meeting structure and the process of elucidating and improving operations, as well as in the immediacy and focus demonstrated in the team meeting process. Similarities in a cross-training emphasis can also exist, in that knowledge of a variety of work area functions does not obviate specialized assignments as was emphasized in the 80/20 specialization section. On the contrary, you can have a broad degree of knowledge gained by hands-on experience, but still primarily operate in ones' strongest performance areas. This variety strengthens the ability to understand and contribute to improving the whole operation, and to knowing what ones' strongest fit is within the process. It also makes it easier to know who to substitute in when another team member is out, either temporarily, or for a longer term assignment. This cross-knowledge allows the team to plan and to know which resources to mobilize, draw-on and / or add.

It should also be pointed out that the Kaizen model, with its emphasis on interchangeability, is one designed for a manufacturing setting. In this type of setting, team member interchangeability is of the utmost importance, and less emphasis is placed on the unique knowledge bases of each member. But consider Peter F. Drucker's comments in *Management Challenges for the 21st Century* (1999). Guerilla Teambuilding **(GT)** relates to teams of *Knowledge Workers*, as Dr. Drucker has coined the phrase. These *Knowledge Workers'* utility to the organization or team is not based upon the tasks they can be trained in, but upon the knowledge that they possess and can bring to a task. These knowledge-based workers are specialized by definition; hence, specialization is inherent in forming teams of *Knowledge Workers*.

Combining the 80/20 pairing practices discussed earlier with the Kaizen model does in some sense, then, create a hybrid model. This hybrid model adjusts the strengths of each to form an ultimate fit to a new type of process. This new process attempts to realize, as Drucker discussed, the excessive potential for productivity of the *Knowledge Worker*. The **(GT)** model draws on the rich foundations of both sets of practices to form such a hybrid.

Resource Materials

Websites

American Psychological Association	www.APA.org
Center for Creative Leadership	www.ccl.org
College of Executive Coaching	www.executivecoachcollege.com
Consulting Psychologists Press	www.cpp.com
Consortium for Research on Emotional Intelligence in Organizations	www.eiconsortium.org
Emotional Intelligence Services Global	www.EISGlobal.com
International Coaching Federation	www.coachfederation.org
J. F. Zagotta & Associates, LLC	www.jfzassoc.com
Multi Health Systems	www.mhs.com
Professional Coaching and Mentors Association	pcmaonline.com
RHR	www.rhrinternational.com
Towers Perrin Forester & Crosby	www.towersperrin.com
Kaizen Institute	www.kaizen-institute.com

Resource Materials

References

Emotional Intelligence

Emotional Intelligence by Daniel Goleman. New York, NY: Bantam Books, 1995

Working With Emotional Intelligence by Daniel Goleman. New York, NY: Bantam Books, 1998

Primal Leadership by Daniel Goleman, Richard Boyatzis, Annie McKee. Boston, MA: Harvard Business School Press, 2002

Flow

Flow by Mihaly Csikszentmihalyi. New York, NY: Harper Perennial, 1991

MBTI and Type

Introduction to Type by Isabel Briggs Myers. Palo Alto, CA: Consulting Psychologists Press, 1998

Do What You Are by Paul D. Treiger, Barbara Barron-Treiger. New York, NY: Little, Brown, 2001

Business Application

Dr. Deming : the American who Taught the Japanese Quality by Rafael Aguayo. Secaucus, NJ: Carol Publishing Group, 1990

Gemba Kaizen : A Commonsense, Low-Cost Approach to Management by Masaaki Imai. New York, NY: McGraw-Hill, 1997

Kaizen, the Key to Japan's Competitive Success by Masaaki Imai. New York, NY: Random House Business Division, 1930, 1986

Management Challenges for the 21st Century by Peter F. Drucker. New York, NY: HarperCollins Publishing, 1999

OHIO Application

Driven to Distraction by Edward M. Hallowel, John J. Ratey. New York, NY: Pantheon Books, 1994

Resource Materials

End Notes

[i]   As a psychologist, I have been trained to use statistical decision models that provide a "cut-off" point that indicates which results actually pose a significant difference and which simply pose a slight variation from the average. Psychologists usually like to use the 95% level as a standard "cut-off" to indicate that something poses a significant difference from what is expected. A piece of data must be 95% different from the usual results (of running a certain test, or observing a particular behavior) to be considered significantly different from the average. The 95% standard is a rather high one for use in decision processes for the average work setting, however, where you don't require this same degree of certainty, but need to know if an issue is just the "same old thing," or if a situation warrants taking action.

[ii]   Diamond Star Motors is a joint venture between Mitsubishi and the former Chrysler Motors based in Normal, IL. The plant manufactures the Plymouth Laser and the Mitsubishi Eclipse (the plant also made the former Eagle Talon). The initial hiring of the plant workers was conducted though a joint venture between the consulting firm of Towers, Perrin, Forester, & Crosby and the Illinois Job Services Corps. TPF&C was contracted to develop an assessment system that would present candidates who possessed skills the parent companies believed would allow them to be successful in a Japanese style manufacturing environment. The initially selected employees trained at a Mitsubishi manufacturing facility in Japan for several months prior to beginning their assignments at the Normal, IL plant. I worked as an independent contractor hired by TPF&C to be a member of an assessment team that helped to develop and implement an assessment center, the purpose of which was to fulfill this employment screening function.

[iii]   This is done as opposed to a hit-or-miss, natural setting approach. Usually it's a miss with many of our clients. Scenarios that occur in natural settings — such as school, a Little League team, or the Boys' and Girls' Clubs — are not always successful for them. These are all fine organizations, but they are not set up to provide the individualized attention that our clients require, nor should they be.

183255

Made in the USA